RACK TOYS

NEW

Nacelle Publishing Presents

Rack Toys
Cheap, Crazed Playthings

By Brian Heiler

Edited by: Rob Chatlin

Design Advisor: Stephen Leach

Painting: Matt Patterson

The Author wishes to thank the following people
in no particular order:

Michelle, Dean and Amy Heiler for
being so supportive and understanding.

My grandmother Elizabeth for giving me so
many two dollar bills for "junk" as a kid. I miss
you.

My Entrepreneurial Parents
Marvin Azrak
Elliot Azrak
Aaron Ber
Bill Frost
Rob Chatlin
Ray Miller
Bryan Ain
Jason Lenzi
Robyn Adams
Mike Jimenez
Shannon T Stewart
Mark Huckabone
Steve Fink
Rich Mayerik
Brian Volk-Weiss
Jeff Smith (koolstuff.ca)
John Scolari
Keene Silfer
Hake's Americana (hakes.com)
Todd Sheffer
Corey LeChat
Ed Leung
John Scoleri
Steve Moore
Stephen Leach
Rob Kelly (fireandwaterpodcast.com)
Bruce Zalkin
Steven C Stolk
Mike Heddle (bountyhuntertoys.com)
Matt Jaycox
Dan Hunter (terrortrap.com)
Matt Patterson (monstermatt.com)
Ray Castile (thegalleryofmonstertoys.com)
Will McGowan (toltoyskid)
Chris Franklin
David Lockwood
Chris Hummell
Variety Product Sales
And Lamb & Pickles

NACELLE PUBLISHING
Rack Toys 2nd Edition

Table of Contents

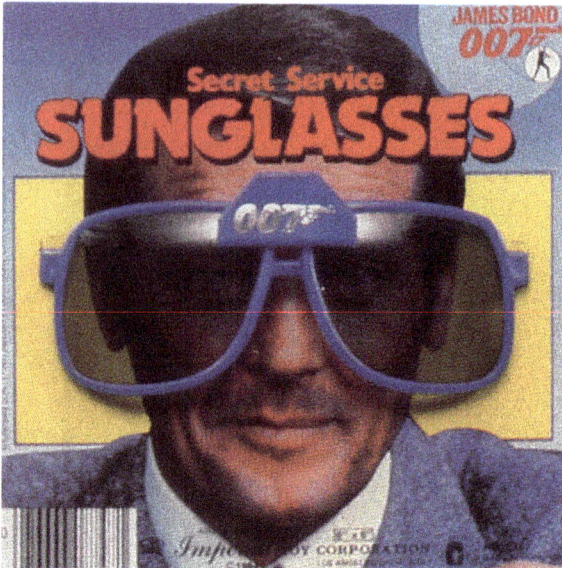

Introduction by Jason Lenzi

There are two things I need to share with you immediately in this introduction. One is that when it comes to pop culture, I believe in the interconnectedness of all things. You know, that magical combination of being in the right place at the right time and then doing the right thing, and those secret handshake moments that come when you least expect it. The other slice of fried gold that I need to share, is that Brian Heiler has a time machine. At least I think he does, because it's the only explanation for how he takes us on such amazing adventures.

If you're actually reading this introduction, there's a better than 50% chance that you're already familiar with Rack Toys. But just in case you're not, I'll give you a quick definition. They're the licensed, and often unlicensed, toys that inhabit that nether world between the serious output of Kenner, Mattel, Hasbro and their ilk, and the generic drug store toys that are meant to satisfy the least discerning kid on the block. Their call signs are Ja-Ru, Nasta and Imperial, and they're marvelous. Their heyday was the 70s and early 80s, and it seems that every TV series, film and comic book character that was prominent in that time frame got the Rack Toy treatment. There's something oddly and beautifully ironic that toys that were meant to placate children for an afternoon and fall apart within hours can fetch such high prices today.

But let's go back in time a bit. I first stumbled across Plaid Stallions, the website Brian runs that celebrates all things 70s toy catalog related, several years ago. After spending an inordinate amount of time on it, I sent him a note telling him how much I loved poring over what he'd obviously put a lot of effort into. He sent a reply a few days later thanking me, but also letting me know that he had JUST picked up Bif Bang Pow!'s Flash Gordon movie action figures several days before he got my note, and returned the compliments. See? The Interconnectedness of all things. The secret handshake of a shared passion. It's all coming together.

For months after wards I sort of got swept up in the Plaid Stallions madness, studying the gorgeous catalog pages of rack toys that took me back to a special place and time and the amazing vintage toy store photos Brian has acquired over the years. I so wanted to be a part of it all, that I sent in pictures of my young self and Darth Vader for the 'Mall Appearance' section, and have contributed not one, but TWO entries to 'Coloring Book Theater'.

Now, as of this book's publication, Brian and I have never actually met, but we've gotten to know each other well through emails, texts and epic phone calls. In fact, he once shared some very intimate shots with me that sent chills down my spine. They were of Brian's office, his Fortress of Solitude if you will, and they illustrated his 70s toy obsession beautifully. When you enter the office, from the right wall to the corner, left along the far wall, and all the way around to the left side of the room, you are confronted with display cases filled to the brim with Rack Toys, Mego action figures and other sundries. Much of the content, some counter display boxes included, looked just as they did back in the year they were released, only missing the wall mounted racks they would have hung off.

It is an impressive collection, but it struck me that it was so much more than just plastic memorabilia. It was a gateway to another time. You and I know the feeling we get of holding one particular toy, how it can conjure up the sights and sounds of our youth. My particular Rack Toy sense memory involves a store called Borgstrom Pharmacy in St. Paul, Minnesota. It was a one stop shop for marketing and prescriptions, and when I went with my mother or father, I would head to the far wall of the store. There is where I did MY shopping, where those crazed plastic playthings lived amongst the squirt guns and coloring books. Lots of money must have been spent there over the years, but it was nothing compared to the priceless joy the purchases brought. The store is long gone now, but I'll be damned if I can't *still* smell its interior and visualize its layout. There were other stand alone toy stores of my childhood: KIDS and Woolworth's in the Maplewood Mall, Storkville in West St. Paul and of course, the many Children's Palace locations. I would give anything to just go back to that time, and visit those places, and have that feeling of wide eyed wonder again. But that would take a time machine, right? And we all know they don't exist.

Well, I'm not sure that's true. As I mentioned earlier, I'm convinced Brian Heiler has one. See, for me, getting back is all about sense memory, associations and the pieces themselves. So when Brian goes in that office and looks around, it's about as close as anyone's ever going to get to actually going back to those wonderful places they used to visit to get their cheap toy fix. And this book is the next best thing. I know people that think high school was Nirvana, or their 20's was the best time ever, or that prescribe to the notion of "be here now", that this moment in time is the best things will ever be. (I try and live by that as much as I can, because I do think it's healthiest). But for me, that glorious time of 1976-1982 or so is the best it'll ever be. The TV shows, movies, music, sights, sounds, smells and yes, toys, have stayed with me throughout my life and continue to influence it in the many avenues I've explored professionally. (If you're paying attention, you'll probably notice some of the Bif Bang Pow! output tries to emulate our childhoods a bit).

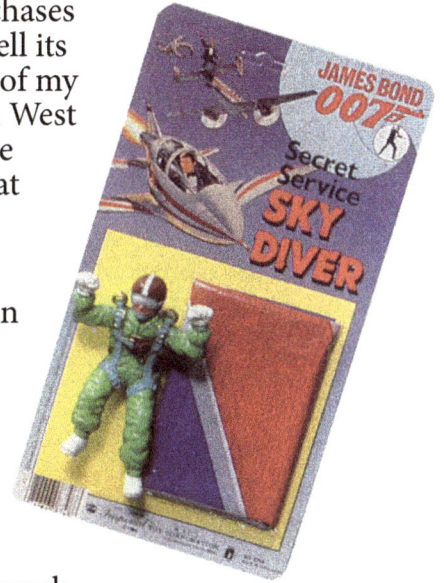

Brian himself has a passion for these things that is inspiring. Any of us that have pursued something as a hobby or business purely for the love of it or because we've been cursed since childhood to never take the safe route can attest to that. Crossing realities, he's even brought a 70s toy to life, his PS mascot, Brick Mantooth, as an 8" retro action figure. He's out there flying the flag, cataloging these things for OUR pleasure. And what's more, he's STILL a seeker. As bountiful as this tome is and as thorough as the PS site gets, Brian continues to discover new oddities that he'd never known existed. (Bizarre recent finds like *Matt Houston*, *Mr. Smith* and *Manimal* come to mind. I mean, *Mr. Smith*? It ran for like, 6 episodes or something. Who could have had the foresight to think *that* was gonna be a hit at the 5 and Dime?) So I know this won't be the only edition of this book we get, there's just way too much stuff out there.

And so to the book. It's a fascinating study. As you flip through it, you'll find a mixture of "I had that!!" moments, followed by just as many "I had NO IDEA that made that!!" moments. And by the time you're finished, you'll be asking, "Hey, how come they never made a Rack Toy for (insert the name of a late 60s-early 80s property here). The beauty of THAT is, they just might have, and the man who'll no doubt unlock that mystery for you is Brian Heiler. And the familiarity of its contents will take you back in time as expected. So here's to the rack toys, the bizarre plastic playthings that were never meant to be kept or treasured, but to get an afternoon's use out of and then forgotten. I, for one, am glad this book exists, the first of it's kind. A reference for a cherished corner of our childhoods, and guide to future collecting. A carry along time machine.

Jason Lenzi is a Televison producer, popular voice over artist, co founder of the toy company "Bif Bang Pow!" and co-host of the popular podcast "Pod Stallions" (www.podstallions.com). The author is particularly envious of his mint on card James Bond sunglasses.

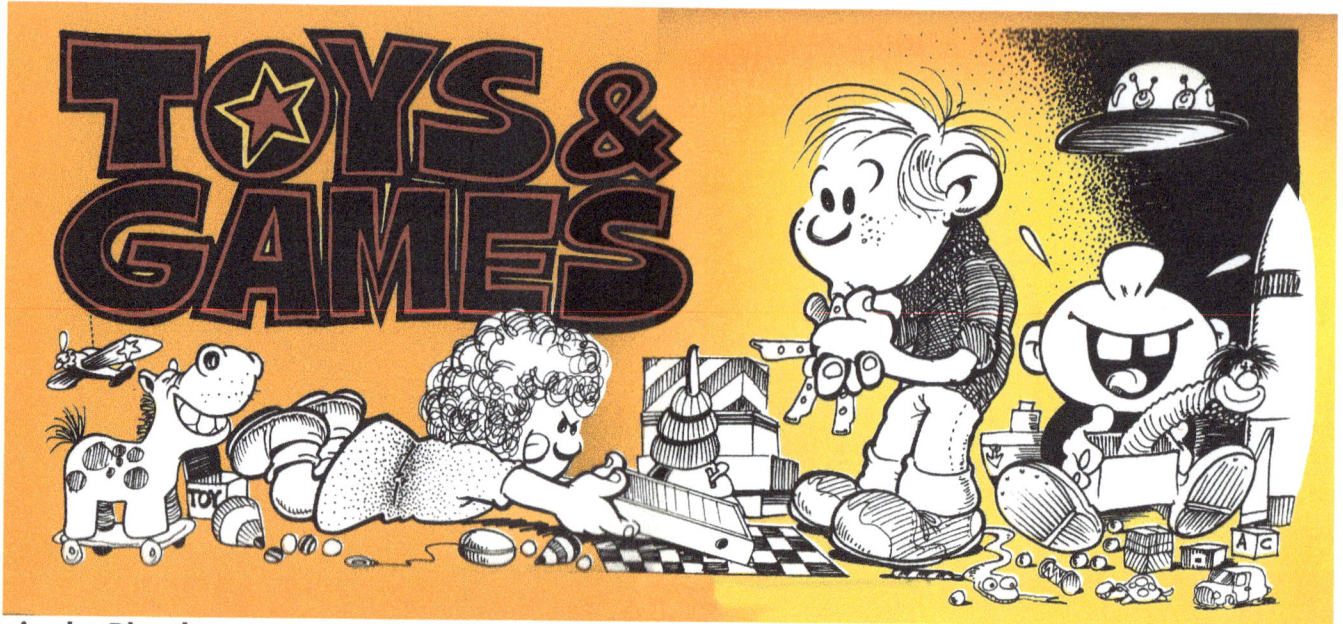

It's in the Blood

Dad sold toys. Well, that's not entirely correct, he was in the 1970s what's commonly known as a "**Rack Jobber**" and sold lots of things: model kits, panty hose, even diaper pins, but being a child at the time the only thing I ever cared about were the toys; although I will admit the lady on the pantyhose package intrigued me.

The toys were either close outs from a few years earlier or Rack Toys, the kind of low cost items you would see at the pharmacy or drug store, but rarely at a dedicated toy store.

The family business was to service the many franchised and independent variety stores in Ontario, Canada and keep their aisles full of low priced impulse items and sundries.

My childhood was filled with afternoons in the family warehouse pouring over toy industry and Hong Kong trader magazines and weekends putting together "variety packs" of different items we would ship to retailers.

At one point, my Dad even opened a "5 and 10" type store to see which products sold best. If a panel of yo-yo's sold well, he'd know they were the hot item and would triple his orders.

Buying trips meant Saturday mornings strolling industrial units filled with various water pistols, knock off monster items and other bric-a-brac all neatly tagged with prices by the gross. It's a lot like going to a toy show now, just a whole heck of a lot cheaper.

This book is the result of an unusual, but by and large happy childhood, and I hope it shows the utter joy a sometimes thoughtlessly made hunk of plastic can bring.

Brian Heiler

PS I published Rack Toys in 2012 and it was one of the best things I ever did. I didn't get rich but I grew as a human being and made many new friends as a result. If you have an aspiration in this life, do it, don't listen to naysayers, just go for it. I'm so happy I took this risk, you should too.

Above:
The funky header card used for the family business to promote toy sections in stores.

Next Page:
A display at a "Mac's Milk" store set up by my father in 1974. Note the orange peg board.

Chapter One
Comic Action Heroes

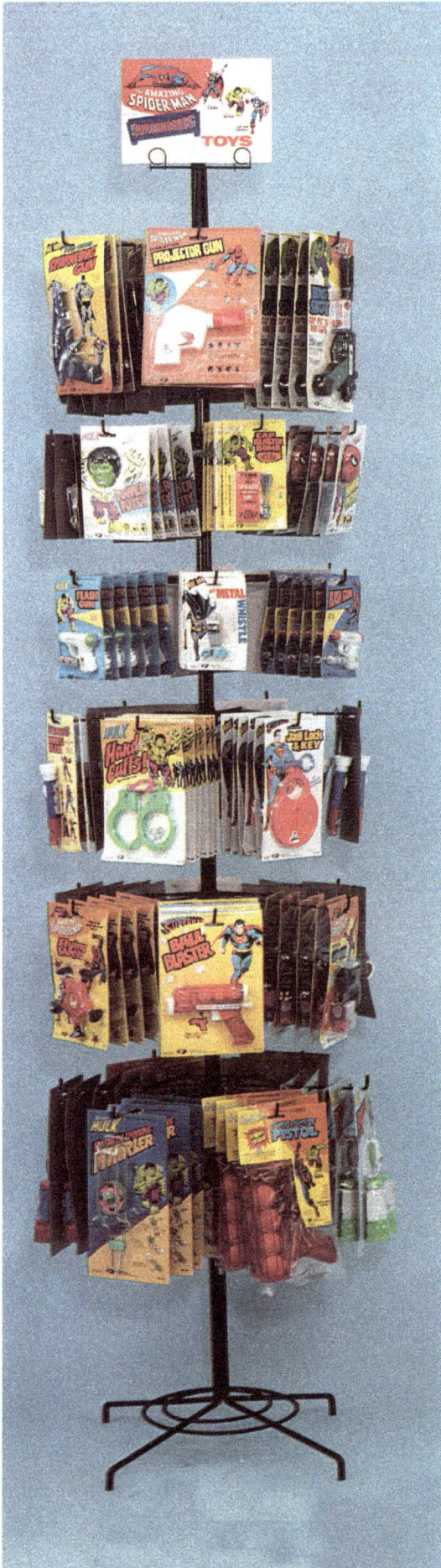

Cash and Capes

Ever since Superman leapt onto the scene in 1938, he has left behind a wake of licensed merchandise. The popularity of caped crusaders transcends the genre, and their imagery has been used to sell almost everything from vitamins to underpants, to dishware and beach towels . Where they excel however, are in the selling of rack toys.

Ironically, the golden child of licensed Superhero products is one that has no superpowers at all.

Batman, with his never ending array of gadgetry and vehicles, is a toy maker's dream. No matter how ludicrous or strange the item, it could be hanging in the Bat Cave somewhere.

In fact, the modern boom for Superhero merchandise began in the 1966 when the "Batman" television series debuted. Since that time, low cost Superhero rack toys of some form have rarely been out of production.

Many Superhero rack toys are simply a pasting of a new heroes' head on an existing Batman item. Characters like Spider-Man who didn't drive in the comics were given their own cars, boats and helicopters that looked strangely familiar. These sorts of things are cost cutting maneuvers that resulted in healthy sales. Kids aren't as concerned with comic book canon as they are with having fun.

Superhero merchandise would find a new renaissance in the 1970s, buoyed by reruns of "Batman" and the new "Super Friends" cartoon series. One of the bigger companies to capitalize on this trend would be Azrak-Hamway International (AHI) who would spend the better part of the decade releasing an explosion of merchandise, ranging from the practical to the very unusual.

Other companies such as Gordy International, Fleetwood Toys, Ja-Ru, Imperial Toys, Lincoln International and Larami would also offer various Superhero goodies, sometimes all in the same year.

Today, even in the wake of billion dollar block buster comic book films, Superhero rack toys are still present in dollar stores to this very day.

Left:
A Superhero display from Gordy International, featuring a slew of completely unheroic items such as whistles, pop guns, hand cuffs and cap bombs.

This 1967 Superman Watergun by Multiple Toymakers cleverly uses its card art to explain why Superman would need to carry such an item: to squirt away Kryptonite.

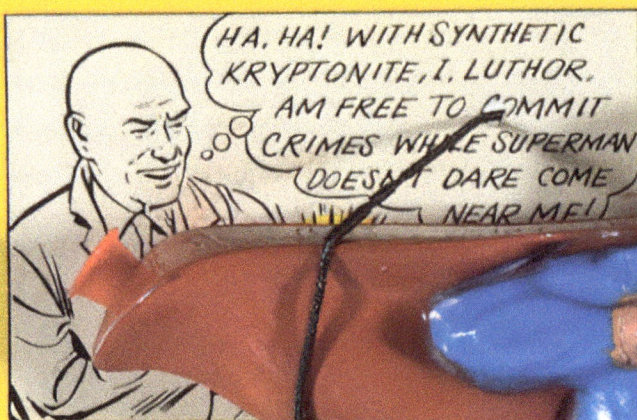

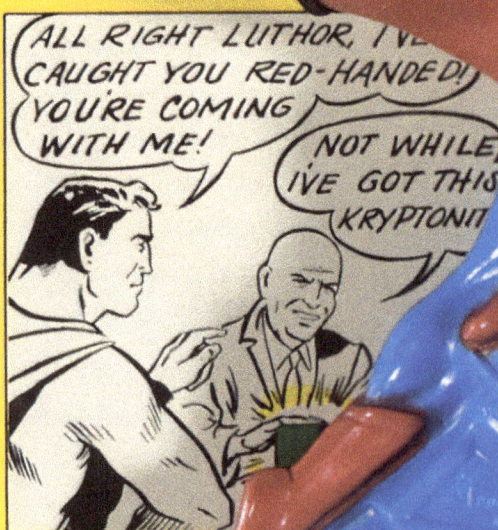

Superman may well be the first Superhero to receive toy licensing, however his abundance of natural talents and lack of accessories does make it a challenge.

SUPER BRAIN TEASER

SLIDING PUZZLE PUZZLE GLISSANT
PUZZLE
UN DÉFI À RELEVER

SUPERMAN

TM & © DC Comics Inc. 1978

©1977 AMERICAN PUBLISHING CORP., Watertown, MA 02172
MADE IN HONG KONG
FABRIQUE AU HONG KONG

4620

Above:
An APC Superman sliding puzzle (1977)

OFFICIAL
SUPERMAN
ZING WING

SUPERMAN

Above:
A Superman parachuute figure from Italy (Manufacturer unknown).

Right:
1974 Superman Zing Wing from AHI features some strangely off model artwork of the Man of Steel.

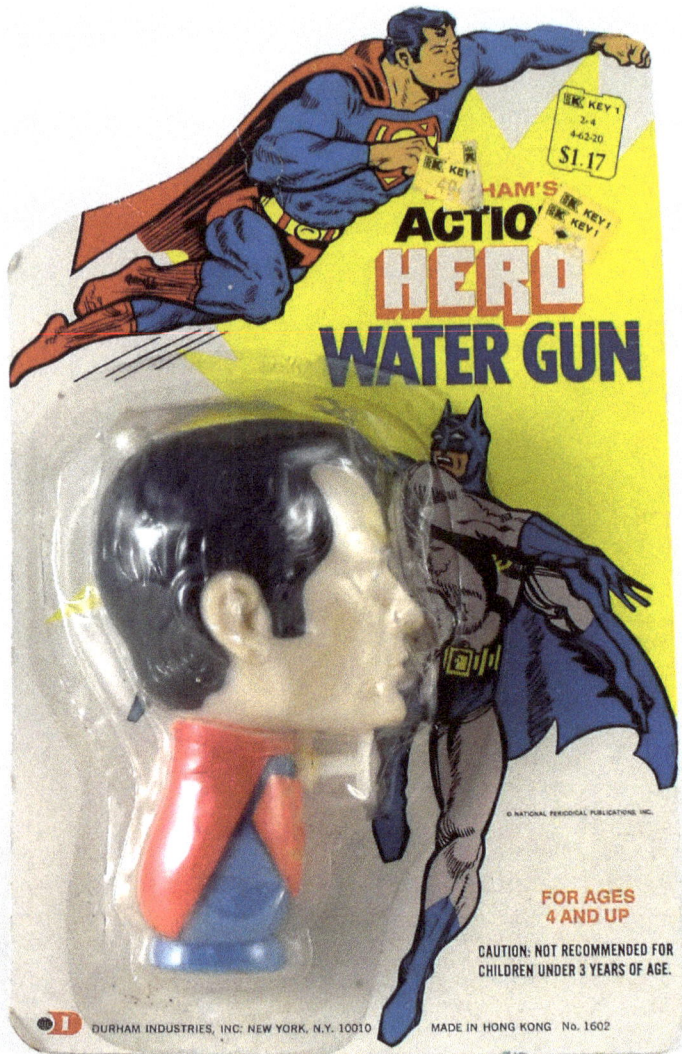

Left:
Have the Man of Steel spit right into the face of your enemies with this 1975 Action Hero Water Gun from Durham Industries.

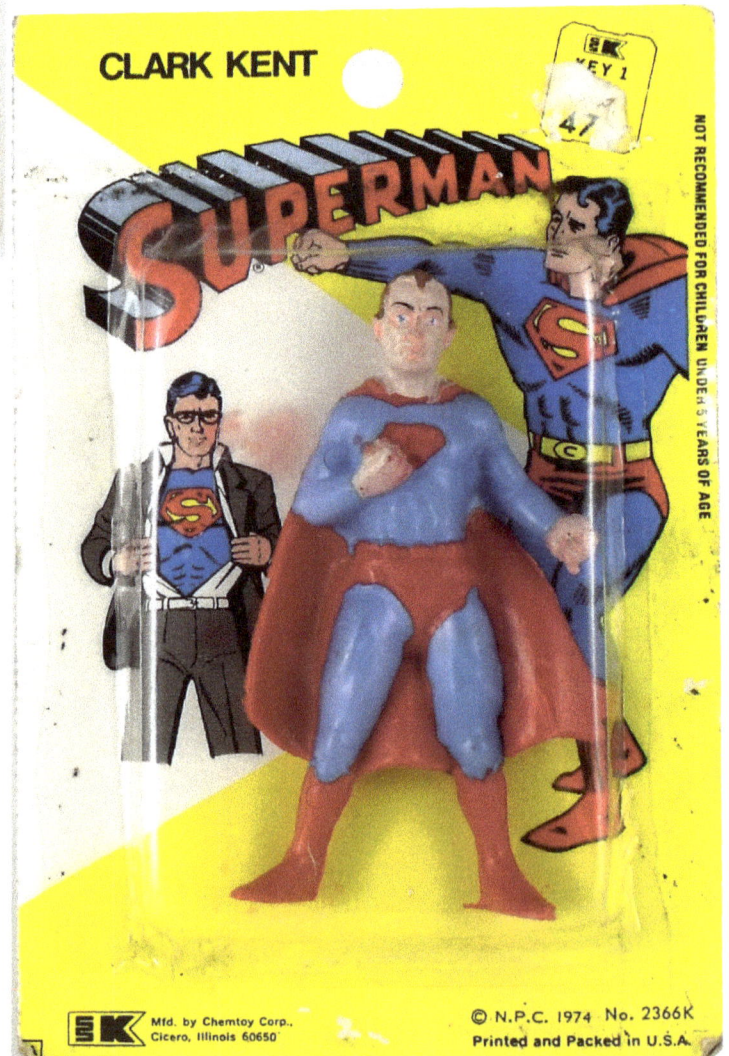

Right:
Chemtoy released these crude figurines of DC comics characters in 1974 but packaged them on eye popping cards.

BATMAN ESCAPE GUN

dual action launcher gun

HOLY HOTFOOT... BATMAN!

KEEP COOL... ROBIN!

complete with 2 Bat Darts and 2 Flying Gadgets

BATMAN

LINCOLN INTERNATIONAL

Holy Cash Cow!

The advent of the 1966 television series "Batman" revealed the character's only superpower; the ability to sell merchandise.

Above:
Lincoln International was one of the first companies to cash in on the 1966 Batman craze with items like this Escape Gun.

Right:
A Lincoln International Batman Seaplane, from 1967, a gift to Batman from Howard Hughes. The majority of Lincoln's output had little to do with the DC Comics character.

USES WATER AS FUEL

OPERATES ON JET PRINCIPLE.

SHATTERPROOF BUTYRATE PLASTIC.

© NATIONAL PERIODICAL PUBLICATIONS, INC., 1966.

BAT MAN AND ROBIN

SPACE PROBE

USES WATER AS FUEL
soars high in the air

$2.50
25/-

LINCOLN INTERNATIONAL

MADE IN NEW ZEALAND.

Above:

A Batman Space Probe made by the New Zealand based Lincoln International.

Right:

This Batman pistol was also sold by Lincoln as "Dr. Who's anti-Dalek Fluid Neutralizer".

BATMAN

A rare store display for the 1967 Consolidated Development Corp Batman Bat Chute figures (carded sample above).

BATMAN™
SUPER FAST ACCELERATOR
BATMOBILE
RECOMMENDED FOR CHILDREN 3 YEARS AND OLDER

FEATURING
NEW
ENERGIZER
POWER PLANT

1229 81
KEY 1
$207

BATMAN © 1979 D.C. COMICS, INC. ALL RIGHTS RESERVED
PACKAGE & DESIGN 1979 AZRAK HAMWAY INT'L INC. NEW YORK, N.Y. 10010
MADE IN THE BRITISH COLONY OF HONG KONG

STYLE NO. 8064

George Barris' design of the Batmobile for the 1966 television series was emulated dozens of times by toy manufacturers. AHI alone made several versions during the 1970s.

Clockwise from the top left: *1976 AHI Catalog Page featuring their line up, Carded Batman Parachutist. In Mexico, the AHI parchute figures were produced under license by Uni Plast. Their version of the Joker is now a regular in my nightmares.*

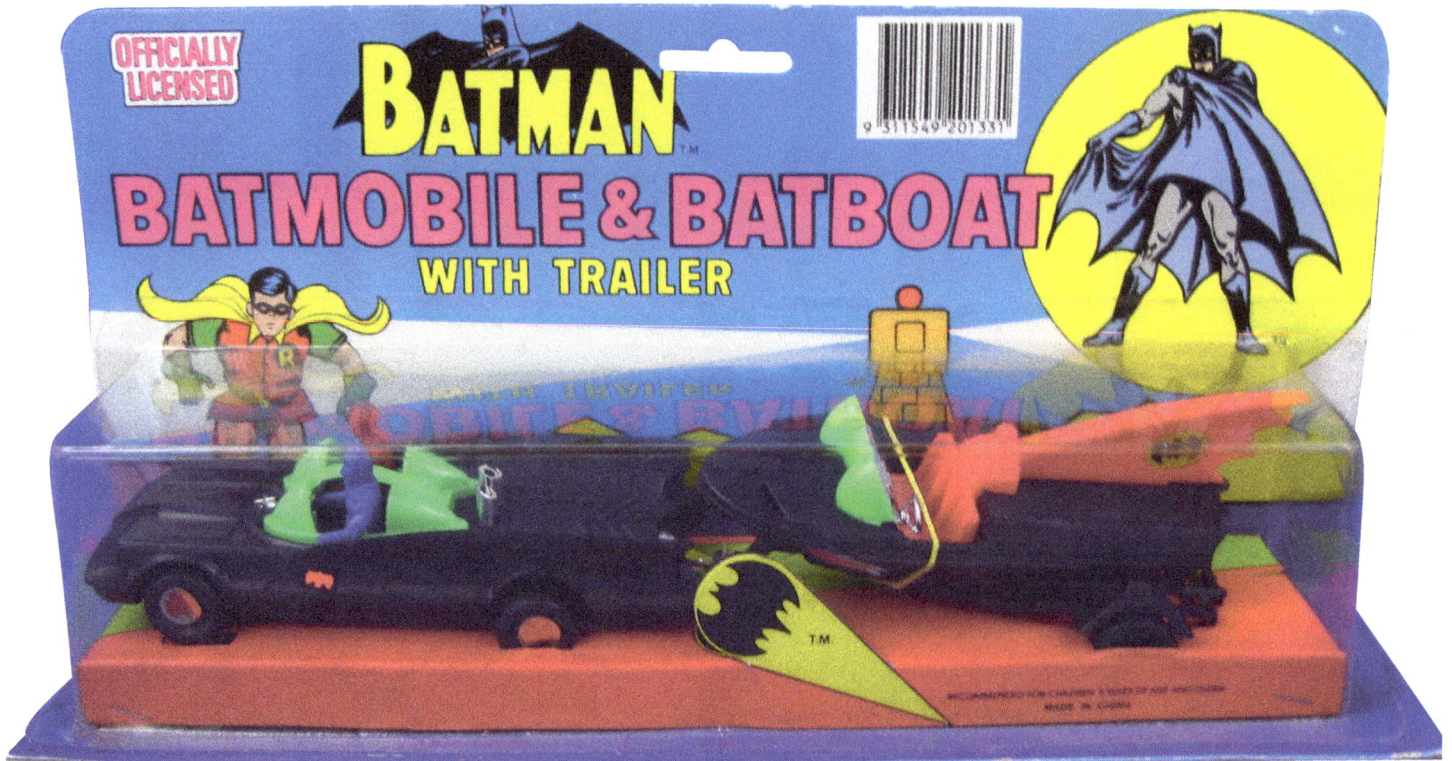

Clockwise from the top:

AHI Batmobile and Batboat, Zoom Batmobile and the Gyro Motorized Batman Stunt Cycle, all from 1975. Just a small sampling of the different "officially licensed" Batman vehicles offered by AHI during the 1970s.

AHI would recycle the Bat Plane model for many other licenses, even the Incredible Hulk.

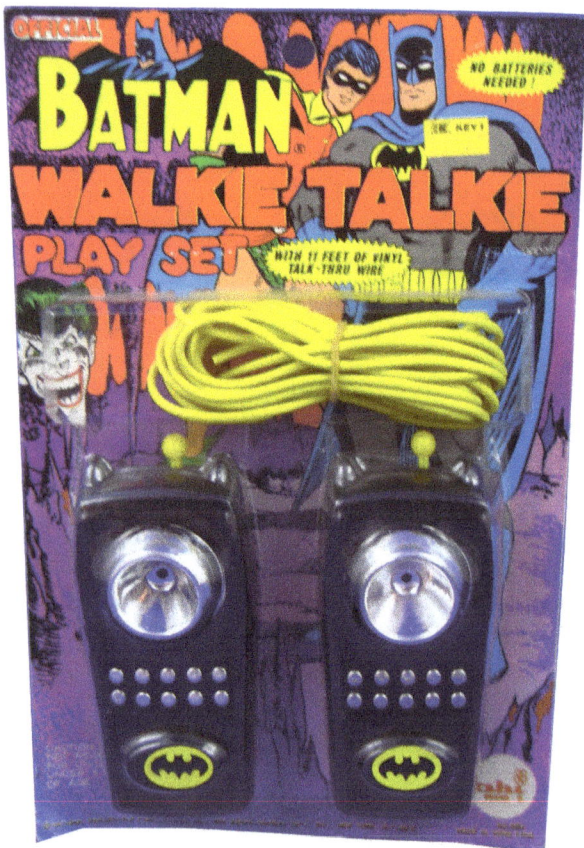

Above Left:

A Batman bendable figure produced for the Australian market by Len Hunter Toys in 1989.

Above:

The Caped Crusader packs heat in this completely out of character 1988 set from Gordy International.

Left:

The eye popping card art for AHI's 1976 Walkie Talkie Play Set.

Right:
One of the more logical items to stem from the Superfriends TV series, the Aquaman Swim Goggle was produced by Sportsotron, which is also a great robot name.

Above:
A Super Friends Robin flashlight produced by Lutece Trading International features a swipe of Alex Toth's brilliant artwork from the TV show.

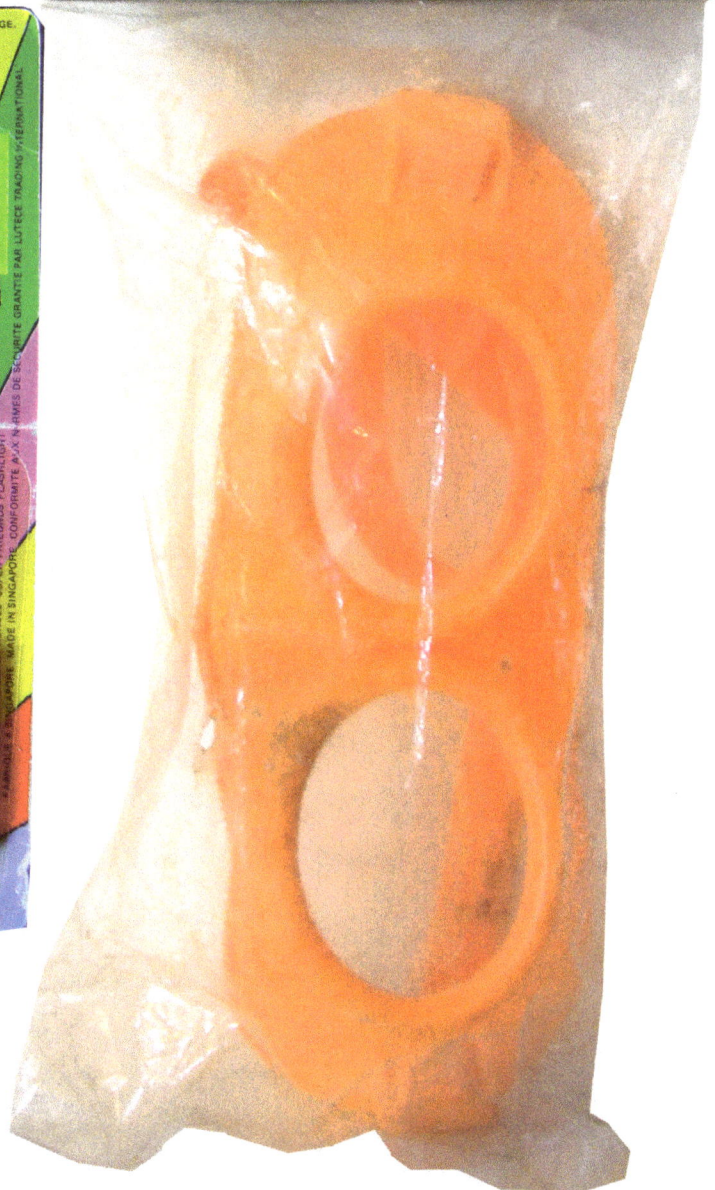

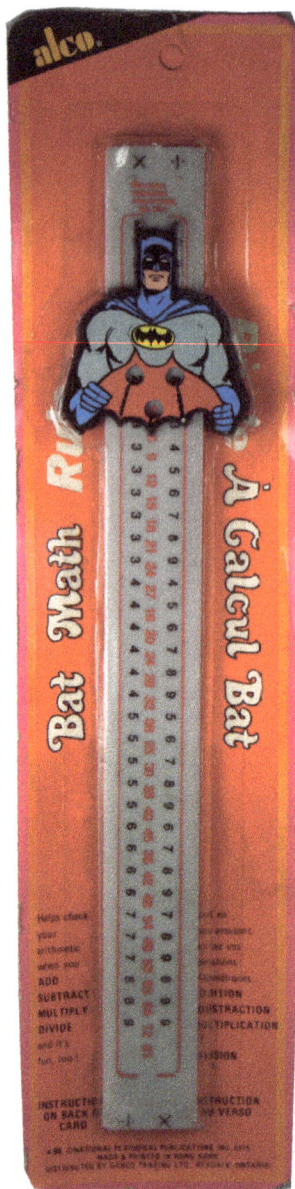

Far Left:
A Shazam! Pencil Sharpener by Alco made learning fun.
Middle:
Bat Math slide rule by Alco.
Above:
A figural Wonder Woman Sharpener also by Alco.
Bottom:
Super Friends pencil sharpener display box (unknown manfacturer)

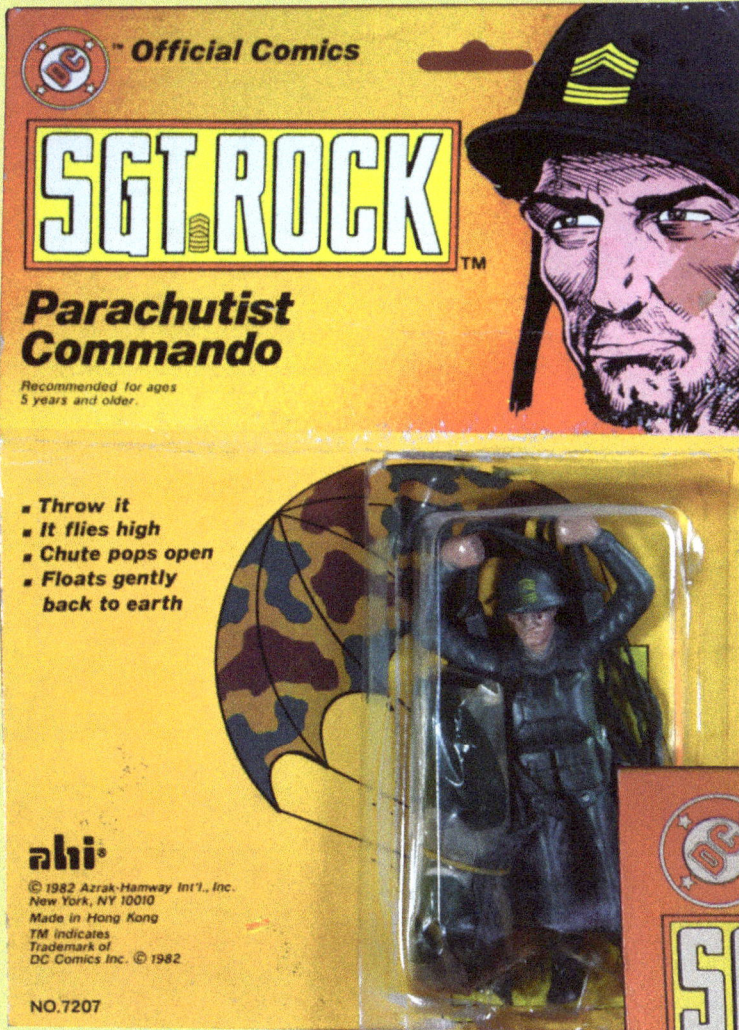

Official Comics

SGT. ROCK

Parachutist Commando

Recommended for ages 5 years and older.

- **Throw it**
- **It flies high**
- **Chute pops open**
- **Floats gently back to earth**

ahi

© 1982 Azrak-Hamway Int'l., Inc.
New York, NY 10010
Made in Hong Kong
TM indicates
Trademark of
DC Comics Inc. © 1982

NO. 7207

SGT. Rock

The hardened war hero from DC Comics received some merchandising when military toys become popular again in the early 1980s.

All of the items produced by AHI were recycled from his leotard wearing friends from DC comics.

Above:

Sgt. Rock Parachutist Commando from 1982 was the last parachute figure produced by AHI.

Right:

The Stunt Cycle also featured some striking Joe Kubert artwork on the package.

Official Comics

SGT. ROCK

Stunt Cycle

- ★ FLIPS
- ★ JUMPS
- ★ SOMERSAULTS
- ★ WHEELIE ACTION

GYRO MOTORIZED

Recommended for ages 5 years and older.

NO NEED TO WIND

NO BATTERIES NEEDED

COMPLETE WITH STUNT RAMP

ahi © 1982 Azrak-Hamway Int'l. Inc. New York, NY 10010
TM indicates Trademark of DC Comics Inc. © 1982

NO. 7289

Thwip!

Next to Batman, Marvel Comic's Spider-Man was the biggest merchandising superstar during the last 30 years. This is despite the fact that his crime fighting arsenal is terribly limited.

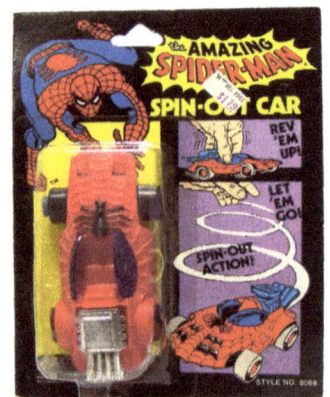

Above:
Spider-Man Web Maker by Chem Toy was an ingenius attempt to replicate the character's signature power, however it usually lasted only for an afternoon.

Above Right:
Spider-Man and the Hulk in a more carefree bubble blowing moment from Larami.

Middle Right:
A Spider-Man pencil sharpener by Alco.

Bottom Right:
The Spider-Car an item actually devised by AHI, that

Clockwise from the top:

 Spider-Man Stunt Cycle, Parachutist, Spidercopter and Spider-man Car are great examples of how AHI captilized on the characters' popularity despite the fact that the majority of these items were not featured in the comic books.

AHI was the first (but not the last) toy company to give Spidey a helicopter.

The Marvel licensing department in the 1970s consisted of one person, rumored to also be a secretary within the company. With that in mind it's easy to see why completely bizarre and totally out of character items like these got produced.

Above:
Spider-Man becames "Dirty Spidey" in this bizzare 1976 set from Larami.

Right:
This Strike Bowling set just proves that Spidey is a regular kid from Queens, also by Larami circa 1978.

Above: *A selection of oddball Superhero items by Gordy International, from their 1980 catalog.*

Below: *Imperial Toys was one of the first to merchandise Stan Lee's new creation Spider-Woman in 1980, albeit in a very traditional "girly" kind of way.*

NO. 8040
SPIDER-WOMAN™
JEWELRY/VANITY SET
2 styles asst.
1 dz to shelf pack
6 dz to shipper   Cd sz: 11¾ x 7
Wt. of shipper: 28 lbs. Cube: 3.0

Marvel's Man of Action

War comics had slipped in popularity by the late 1970s but the recognizable face of Marvel Comics Sgt. Fury helped sell a few green plastic army men regardless.

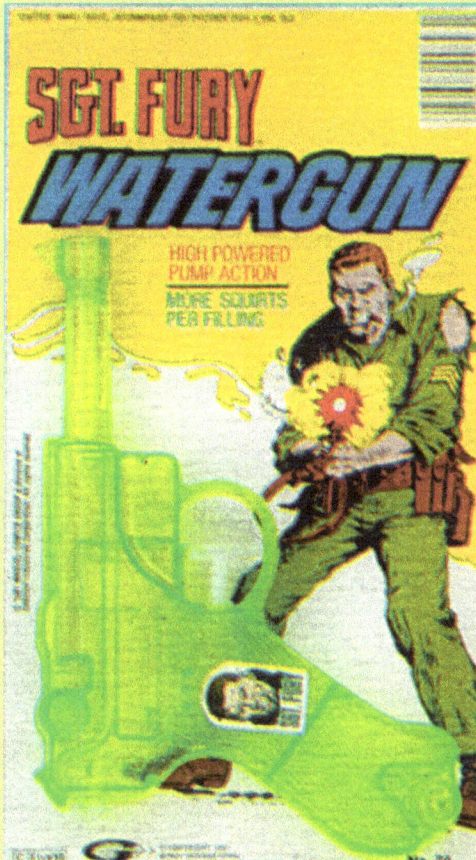

Above:
A curiously German Water Gun courtesy of Gordy International.

Above Right:
Fleetwood Toys sold many green plastic Army Men sets under the Sgt. Fury banner

Right:
Armored Attack by Fleetwood Toys featured some classic Nick Fury stock art by Jack "King" Kirby.

Sentinel of Liberty

Captain America never had the popularity of Spider-Man but the red, white and blue Avenger has seen his share of toy love over the decades.

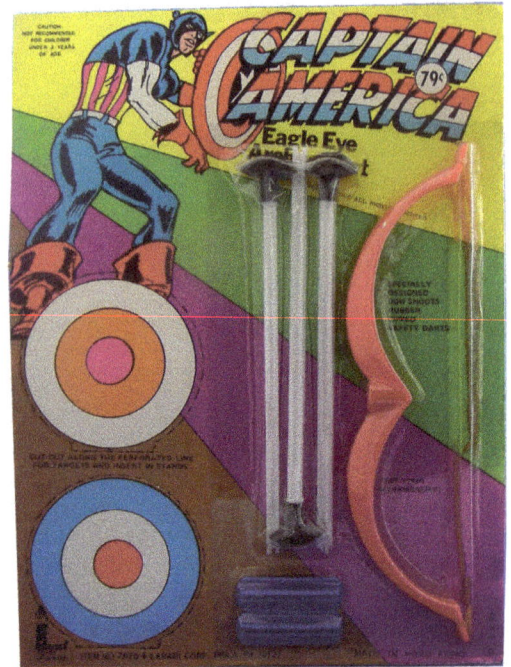

Above:

Captain America Eagle Eye Archery Set produced by Larami in 1979 is a departure for the Avenger who didn't shoot arrows.

Above:

A Captain America Parachutist and Launcher produced by AHI in 1979.

Right:

A Captain America Super-Flex figure produced by Lakeside Toys in 1966.

CHILD WORLD
CHILDREN'S PALACE
419152
OUR LOW PRICE
55

GLOWING
SUPER HEROES™

FLASHLIGHT   BATTERY
INCLUDED

COLLECT
EM ALL !

© 1978 FLEETWOOD TOYS INDUSTRIES
Made in Hong Kong   #21501

fleetwood

Those Other Guys

Many Superheroes recieved their earliest merchandise through Rack Toys as the low cost nature allowed the manufacturers to take risks with lesser known characters who didn't benefit from the same popularity as "A List" characters like Spider-Man and the Hulk.

Left:
Fleetwood's Glowing Super Heroes were simply clever flashlights with great card artwork in 1976.

Bottom :
Imperial Toys 1978 Marvel Super Hero finger puppets were offered both carded and in Display boxes

Left:
AHI proposed a series of Fantastic Four Parachutists in 1979 to correspond with their animated series on NBC that year. It is unknown if these figures ever saw production.

Below:
Ben Cooper selected an interesting assortment of Marvel characters for their Jiggler line in 1980. Red Skull and Doctor Strange hadn't seen much by the way of merchandise prior to this.

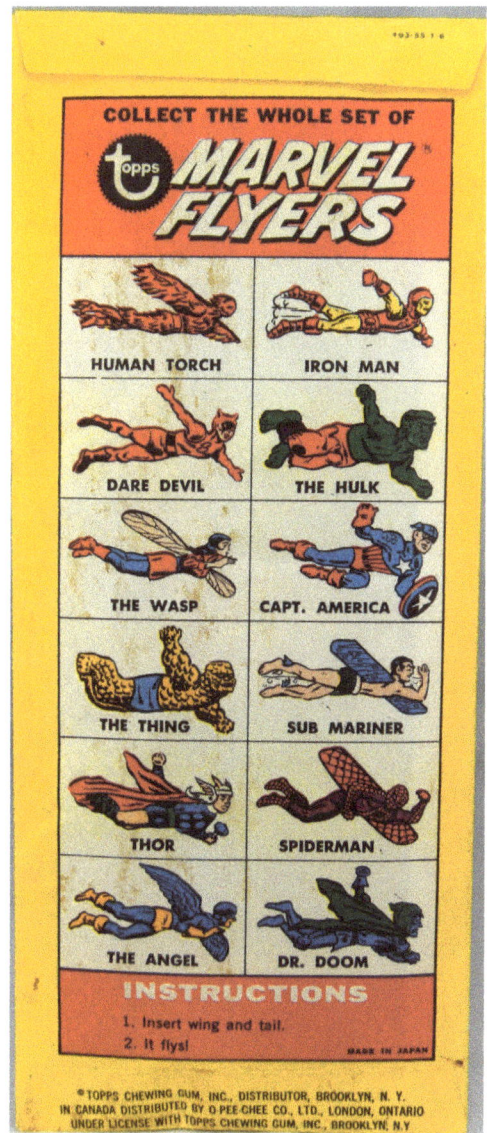

Above Left:

A Fantastic Four Super Car, produced by Fleetwood Toys in 1977.

Above:

Topps Marvel Flyers produced in 1966 are some of the earliest Marvel comics toys.

This Ghost Rider set by Fleetwood Toys in 1977 is now a highly sought after collectible.

The Color of Money

The Incredible Hulk was a late bloomer when it came to merchandise but his selling power rose considerably thanks to his hit CBS Television series in the 1970s.

Despite being essentially a super powered homeless person, many toy companies gave the Hulk an impressive array of gadgets and vehicles that would make Batman jealous.

Above:
A 1979 AHI Hulk Water Gun

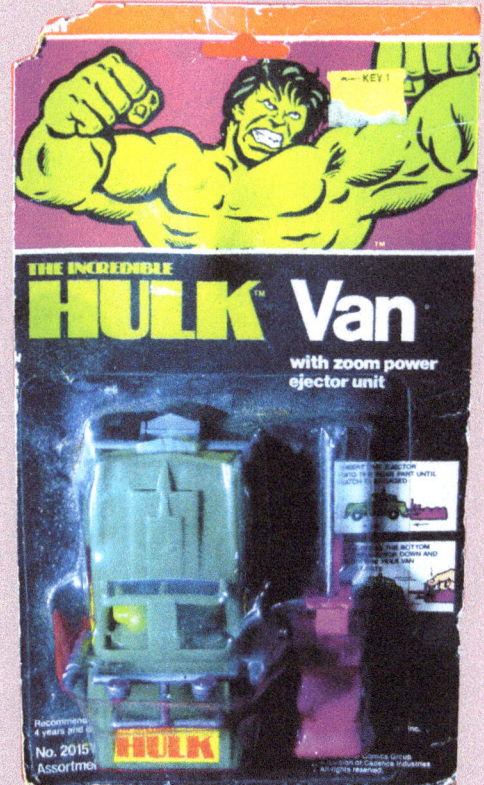

Above:
The 1979 Hulk sky dives into backyard adventures with the AHI Parachutist, a late entry into the series.

Above:
The 1979 Hulk Van is actually a pick up truck but I won't argue with him.

THE INCREDIBLE HULK™ Stunt Cycle

WHEELIES! JUMPS! FLIPS!
No Batteries needed!

Stunt Ramp Included!

No. 2019
Assortment No. 6089

The Incredible Hulk Stunt Cycle by AHI.

No. 7211-6 $1.00
SPECIAL AGENT
PK: 3 doz.
Card Size C 7" x 11¾"

No. 8064-8 $1.29
MOBILE COMMANDER
PK: 1 doz./12 doz.
Card Size C 7" x 11½"

No. 9691-7 $1.00
WALKIE TALKIE
PK: 2 doz./12 doz.
Card Size B 6" x 10"

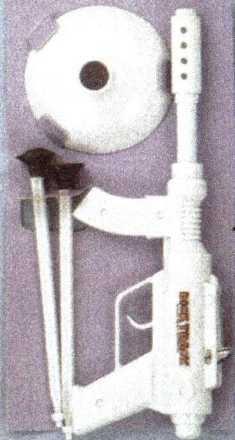

No. 8068-9
DART & CAP GUN
PK: 1 doz./12 doz.
Card Size D 6" x 15¾"

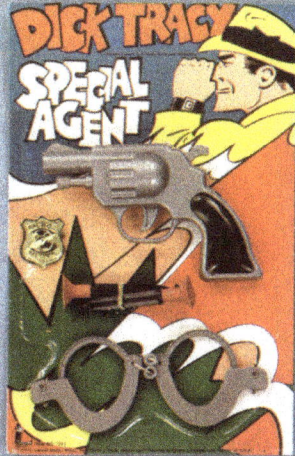

8158-8 $1.29
CRIMEFIGHTERS SET
PK: 1 doz/12 doz.
Card Size B 6" x 9"

No. 3007-2   39¢
3 ASST'D. WATCHES
PK: 3 doz./36 doz.
Card Size A 4" x 7"

No. 9487-0 $1.00
SQUAD CAR
PK: 1 doz./12 doz.
Card Size B 4" x 10"

No. 5027-8   59¢
POLICE RESCUE SQUAD
PK: 2 doz./24 doz.
Card Size B 5" x 9"

No. 6598-7   69¢
DOUBLE SPY GLASS
PK: 2 doz./24 doz.
Card Size B 4" x 9"

No. 7024-3   79¢
COLOR TV MOVIES
PK: 2 doz./24 doz.
Card Size B 4½" x 8¼"

No. 4009-7   49¢
CRIMESTOPPERS SET
PK: 2 doz./24 doz.
Card Size C 4½" x 11½"

No. 7035-9   79¢
WRIST TV
PK: 2 doz./24 doz.
Card Size B 5" x 9"

No. 9518-2 $1.00
CRISIS CONTROL
PK: 2 doz./12 doz.
Card Size B 6" x 9"

No. 5030-2   59¢
COPS & COPTER SET
PK: 2 doz./24 doz.
Card Size A 6" x 9"

No. 8065-5 $1.29
M-16 PELLET RIFLE
PK: 1 doz./12 doz.
Card Size D 4½" x 17½"

This 1976 catalog page from Larami shows that Dick Tracy could still sell police related toys.

37

Right:
Phantom Jet by Imperial Toys in 1975.

Far Right:
More Phantom merchandise by Larami in 1976

No. 9726-1
PHANTOM JET
PK: 2 doz./12 doz./6.76'
Card Size: 7" x 12"

No. 6025-1   69¢
PATHFINDER SET
PK: 3 doz./24 doz.
Card Size A 5" x 7"

No. 7040-9   79¢
CAMERA FLASHLIGHT
PK: 2 doz./24 doz.
Card Size A 5" x 7"

No. 8080-4 $1.29
JUNGLE SET
PK: 1 doz./12 doz.
Card Size B 6" x 10"

No. 8052-3 $1.29
DESERT SURVIVAL KIT
PK: ½ doz./12 doz.
Card Size D 5" x 12½"

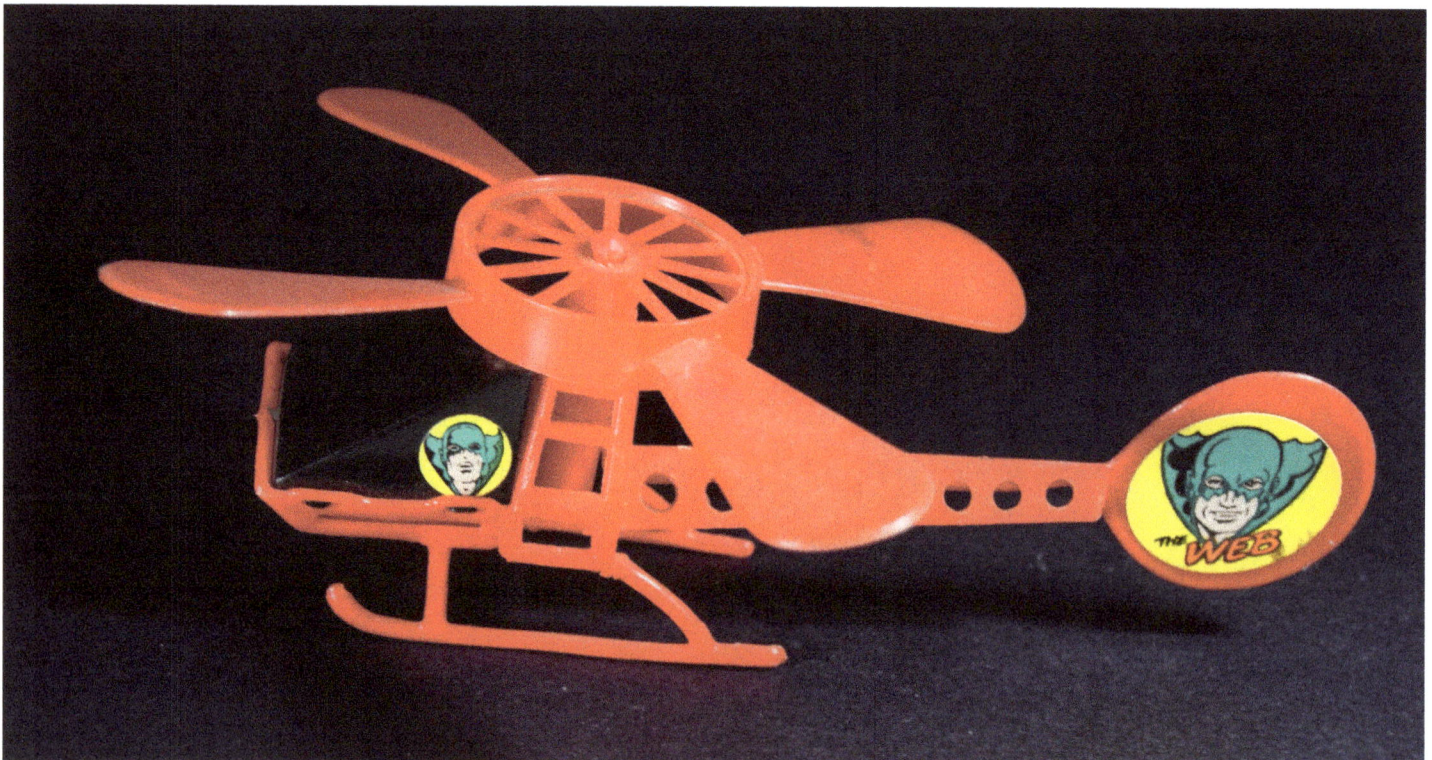

Above:
One of AHI's last licenses was the Archie comics superhero brand *The Mighty Crusaders* in 1983. *This rare copter features their iconic crime fighter The Web.*

38

REMCO

POWER UNLEASHED

AGES 5 AND UP
8102

The World's Mightiest Heroes! ™

MIGHTY CRUSADERS

PARACHUTIST

FLY 'EM HIGH!

GOOD

Remco Mighty Crusaders Parachutists are extremely hard to find in the secondary market.

TOYS, TOYS
& MORE TOYS

MIGHTY CRUSADERS™*
The license that proves that
Might makes right.

Parachutist – Sting, Web
(2 asst)
Item #8102
Pack: Mst. Ctn. 72
Weight: 15 lbs.
Cube: 2.0

Stunt Planes – Sting, Web
(2 asst)
Item #8121
Pack: Mst. Ctn. 24
Weight: 9 lbs.
Cube: 2.5

Helicopter – Sting, Web
(2 asst)
Item #8110
Pack: Mst. Ctn. 72
Weight: 22 lbs.
Cube: 3.6

Walkie Talkie – Sting, Web
(2 asst)
Item #8111
Pack: Mst. Ctn. 72
Weight: 22 lbs.
Cube: 3.0

Water Guns – Sting, Web,
Fox (3 asst)
Item #8116
Pack: Mst. Ctn. 72
Weight: 16.5 lbs.
Cube: 3.0

Saucer Gun – Sting, Web
(2 asst)
Item #8118
Pack: Mst. Ctn. 72
Weight: 16.5 lbs.
Cube: 2.8

Stunt Cycle – Sting, Web
(2 asst)
Item #8109
Pack: Mst. Ctn. 72
Weight: 33 lbs.
Cube: 3.0

*©1984 Archie Comics Publications,
Inc. All Rights Reserved.

Remco had ambitious plans for the Mighty Cursaders in 1985.

Left:
The Shadow Mobile from Madison Imports from 1977 is a retooled AHI Batmobile. The character had a brief resurgence thanks to a DC comic series.

Below:
Shadow Crime Fighter Super Jet, also by Madison Imports in 1977, is yet another item that had a previous life as an AHI Batman item.

FRICTION

THE **Shadow** ®
© MCMLXXVII THE CONDE NAST PUBLICATIONS, INC.
CRIME FIGHTER SUPER JET

RECOMMENDED FOR CHILDREN 3 YEARS OLD AND UP.

Shadow
CRIME FIGHTER

Shadow
CRIME FIGHTER

FRICTION POWER

MADISON IMPORTS, HACKENSACK, N.J. 07601
MADE IN HONG KONG
NO. 2110

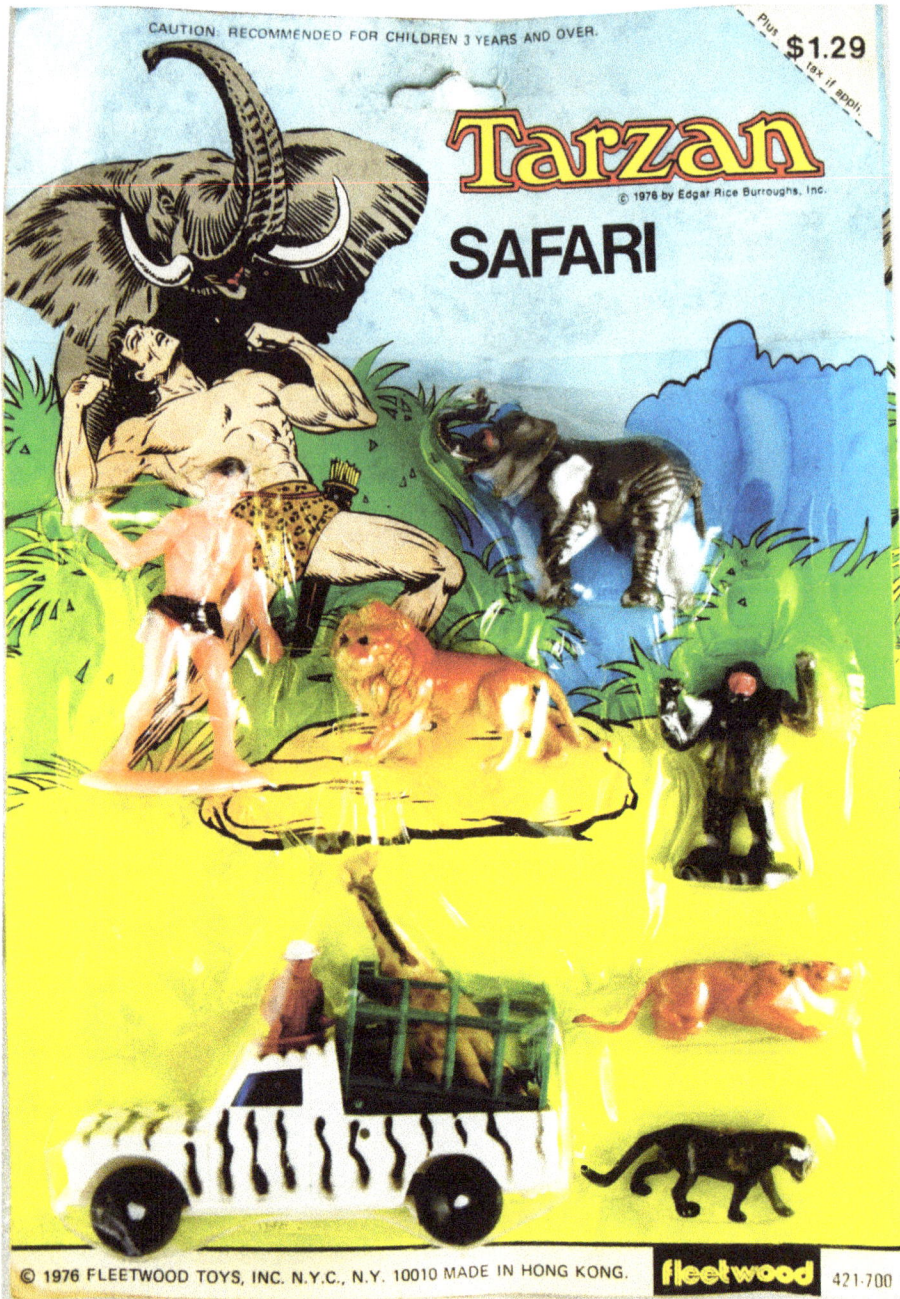

Abovre Left:
A Fleetwood Tarzan Safari set from 1977
Above Right:
Tarzan Jungle Communicators, also from Fleetwood Toys 1977.
Right:
Imperial Toys picked up the Tarzan license in 1980, no doubt due to his popular Saturday morning series by Filmation.

Chapter Two
Spooky Fun

They Did The Mash

Monster and horror related merchandising saw its highest pea[k] in the early 1960s when television syndication packages of clas[sic] black & white horror films turned a generation of children int[o] ghouls.

The boon in popularity helped established Monsters, particula[rly] the characters from Universal Studios, into a viable licensed brand. Many Rack Toy manufacturers worked with the Monst[er] properties over the decades as most retailers saw Monster merchandise as seasonal but perennial money makers.

Above:
In 1979 a company known as Vics reissued smaller versions of the AHI Jigglers on colorful cards.

Below:
A sample of the 1975 Azrak Hamway catalog featuring some of their licensed Universal Monster items.

Above:
A very hard to find Official World Famous Super Monsters Bend 'Ems by AHI.

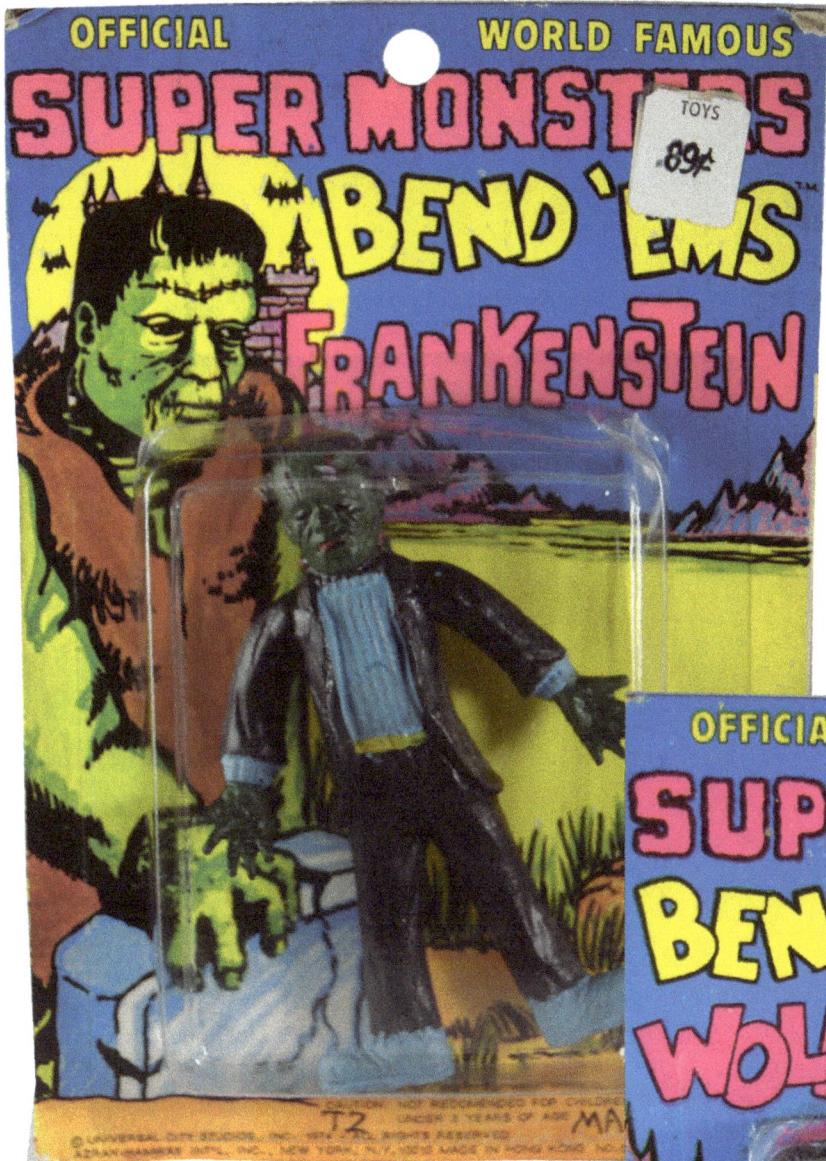

Frankenstein and
Wolfman Bend 'Ems by
Azrak Hamway show the
artistic freedom allowed
in an age before licensing
departments created style
guides for a unified look.

In 1074, AHI sold two styles of these PVC Wiggly figures, the larger versions pictured here were sold in counter top display boxes (overleaf), while slightly shorter versions were sold on blister cards.

WORLD FAMOUS

SUPER
MONSTERS ™

NOT RECOMMENDED FOR CHILDREN
UNDER 5 YEARS OF AGE

NON-TOXIC PAINT

FRANKENSTEIN

WOLFMAN

CREATURE FROM
THE BLACK LAGOON

WORLD FAMOUS

SUPER
MONSTERS ™

NOT RECOMMENDED FOR CHILDREN
UNDER 5 YEARS OF AGE

NON-TOXIC PAINT

FRANKENSTEIN

WOLFMAN

CREATURE FROM
THE BLACK LAGOON

MUMMY

The AHI Monsters

Perhaps one of the biggest boons in Monster merchandise came when Azrak Hamway International (AHI) released a multitude of officially branded Universal Monster product in the early to mid 1970s.

This merchandise included not only lower cost 8" action figures (largely inspired by rival toy manufacturer Mego's line of Super Heroes) but also bendable figures, jigglers, wind ups and water pistols.

While the Official World Famous Super Monsters line only had a brief two year run, they are now actively collected by adults who remember them as children .

Left:
In the United Kingdom, AHI's Dracula figure was sold in a window box and is one of the hardest pieces to find in the series.

Below:
Newspaper ad for the Super Monsters, circa 1976.

Above:
AHI World Famous Super Monster 8" action figures; many variations exist for each figure.

Below:
AHI Super Monsters from their 1975 Catalog. Note that Frankenstein and Wolfman are on the wrong cards.

1.42

WORLD
FAMOUS SUPER

PLACE THEM IN ANY
GRUESOM

The Creature

Dracula

Frankenstein

6126
5-Asst. 8" World Famous Super Monsters
with movable arms & bendable legs
Blistered on card
Carton Pack: 7s Pcs.

MONSTERS !

OSITION !

GRUESOME !

CREEPY !

TERRIBLE !

The Mummy

Wolfman

The Creature

The Mummy

Frankenstein

Wolfman

6050
4-Asst. PVC World Famous Monsters
Display Box
Carton Pack: 72 Pcs.

SUPER MONSTERS

The Lincoln International Monsters

Buoyed by the success of the AHI Monsters, New Zealand based Lincoln International created these unlicensed 8" action figures.

While crude, these low cost figures have become quite popular in collector circles.

Above:
The six Lincoln 8" Monsters figures along with the Girl Victim, a rare catalog exclusive.

Right:
A Count Dracula Figure on its' original blister card and a drugstore newspaper ad.

Next Page:
Box art for "Frankensten" (a misprint) and Mummy figures.

52

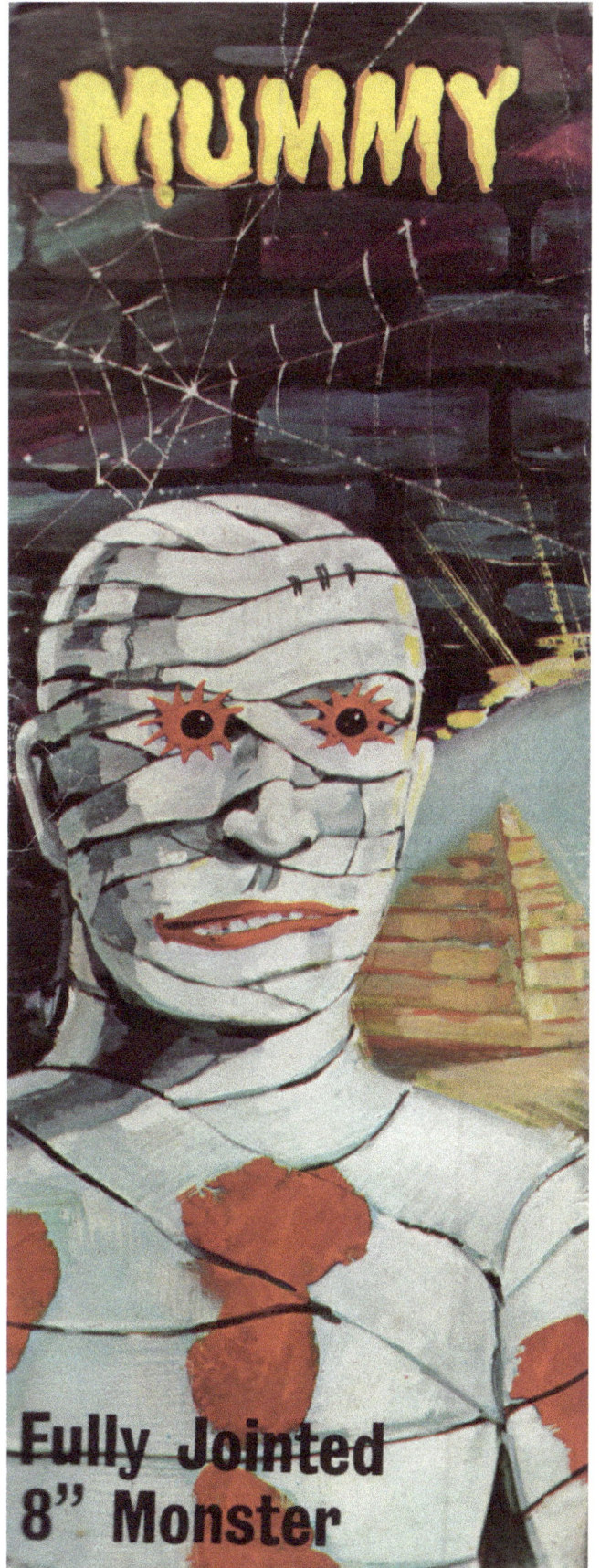

FRANKENSTEN

Fully Jointed
8" Monster

MUMMY

Fully Jointed
8" Monster

Famous Monsters Of Legend

The Tomland Toy Corporation liked to follow trends, but thought it unimportant to pay for a license.

The Famous Monsters of Legend series included two waves of 8 " Legendary monster figures, the second wave featuring glow in the dark heads, feet and hands. Additionally they created a series of wonderful "Super Deformed" type figures. All these characters were l public domain concepts that were clearly based on movie interpretations.

While the first wave of monsters were easily found at K-Mart, the second wave and the super deformed figures seemed to have almost no North American distribution.

Left:
A carded Tomland Famous Monsters of Legend Mummy figure from the second series.

Above:
These smaller Super Deformed figures dubbed "Mini Monsters" by collectors are extremely hard to find.

FRANKENSTEIN

DRACULA

WOLFMAN

MUMMY

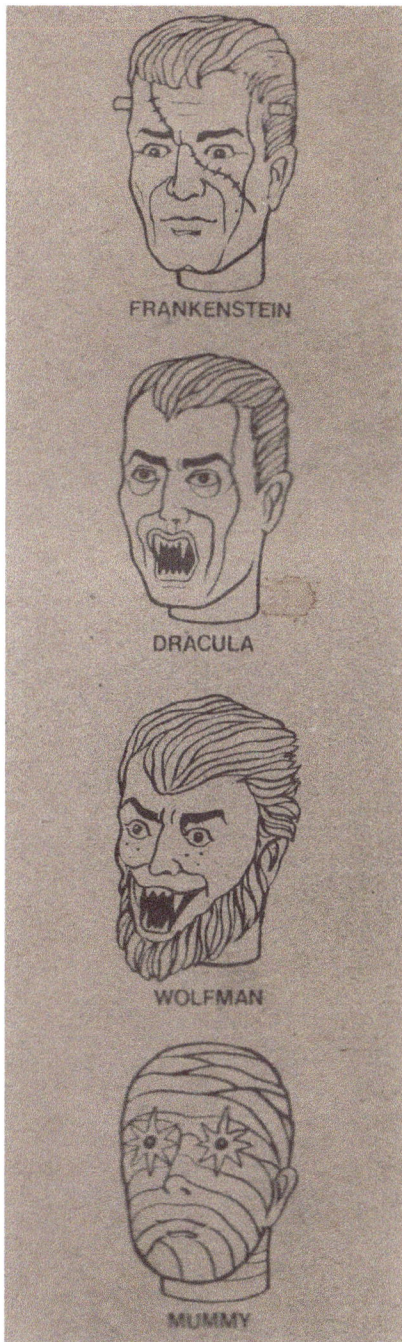

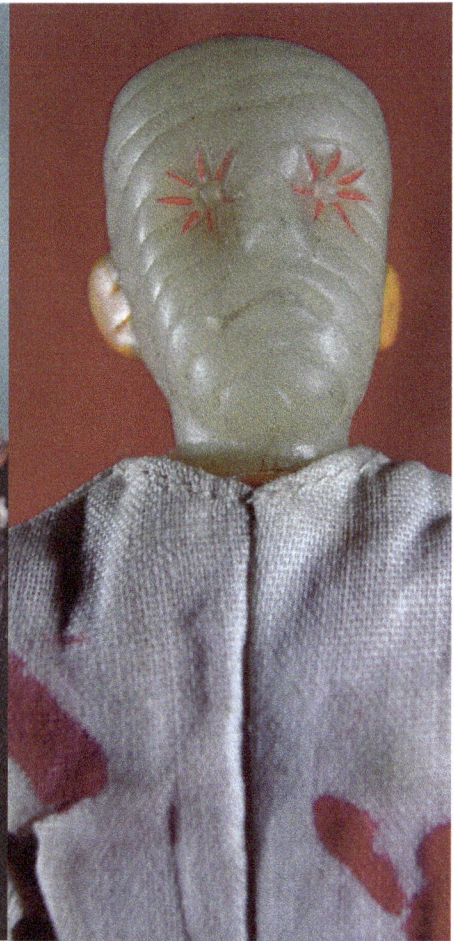

Above:
The backer card artwork for the very rare second wave of Tomland Famous Monsters.

Right:
Close ups of the four elusive glow in the dark classic characters whose look was largely copied from the Lincoln Monsters, sold four years earlier.

LIONEL
1260
STYLE
KEY 1
SKU #
1.25EA
OUR PRICE

GODZILLA
KING OF THE MONSTERS

Bend and Pose into Thousands of Different Positions!

© 1978
© 1978 GLJ Toy ... ng Kong ... et, N.Y. 117... No. 1260

glj
toy co., inc.

GLJ Toys did an admirable job in releasing this Godilla bendy figurine in 1979, even going to the trouble of producing some of the most unique card art of the decade.

NO. 8972 PVC GODZILLA

Stands 6'' tall, with articulated arms, legs and tail   2 dz to display box 20¼ x 11 x 6½   3 dispalys to shipper   Wt. of shipper: 26lbs   Cube: 5.5

Above:

Imperial Toys released several low cost rubber Godzilla figures in 1985 that sold millions.

Below:

Imperial Toys also had the King Kong license which allowed you to reenact a classic battle.

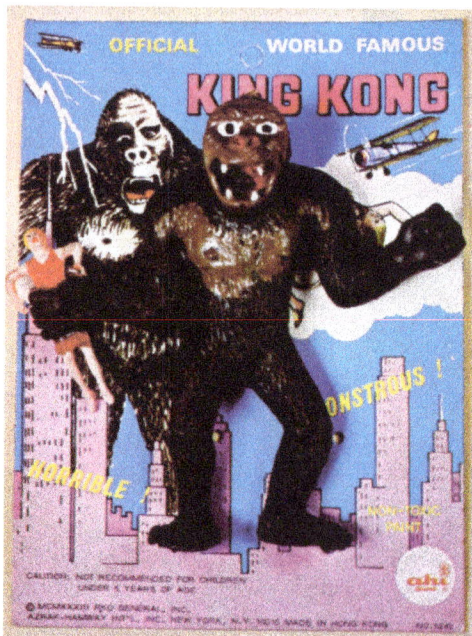

Above:
AHI carded PVC Wiggly of Kong from 1974.

Above:
Carded Kong Bend 'Em by AHI from 1974.

Right:
Imperial King Kong figure from 1986.

Left:
These Monster Glasses provided some spooky generic thrills. Date and Manufacturer unknown.

Below:
The card art for this Mexican made "Kingdom of the Spiders" Rack Toy showed more imagination than the crudely made toys it contains.

These finely sculpted Monster figures were originally made by Louis Marx and Company to captilize on the original Monster craze in the early 1960s. While Mexican bootlegs were produced for years, they were officially reissued some 30 years later by Uncle Milton.

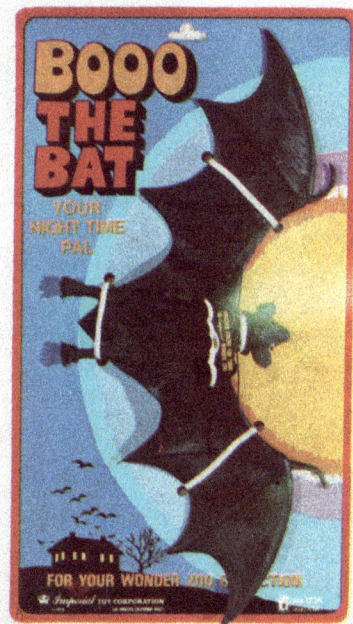

#91   HALLOWEEN FLOOR DISPLAY
Total Retail $61.92
Asst. consists of: 2 doz. # 1237 Boney Benny
                     2 doz. # 1236 Boo the Bat
Packed 1 ea. to shipper
Weight of shipper: 19 lbs.

Above:
 Imperial Toys didn't have to rely on licenses to sell horrors. Their Halloween program consisting of rubber bats, bugs and skeletons and has kept them in business to this day.

Next Page:
A display of Glow in the Dark Space Faces Stickers which have been made availble under many different names over the years.

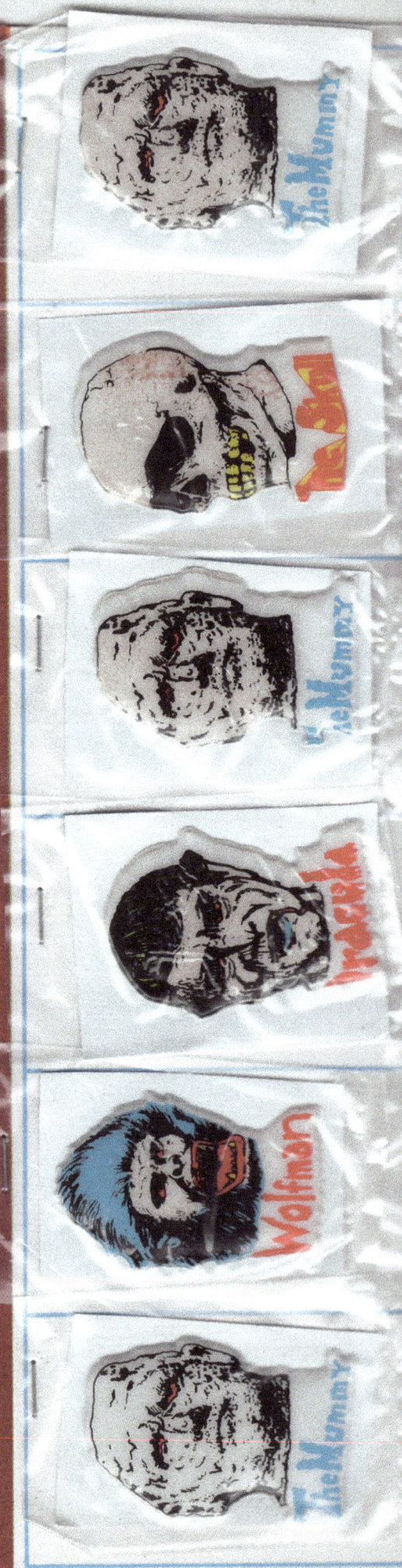

WIND UP SPARKING SUPER MONSTERS LITTLE WALKERS

WIND UP SUPER MONSTERS LITTLE WALKERS SPARKING

WIND UP SPARKING SUPER MONSTERS LITTLE WALKERS

No. 505/3A   MADE IN HONG KONG

These Super Monsters Little Walkers were originally created and sold by AHI but were copied and made available from a number of manufacturers from the 1970s to the present.

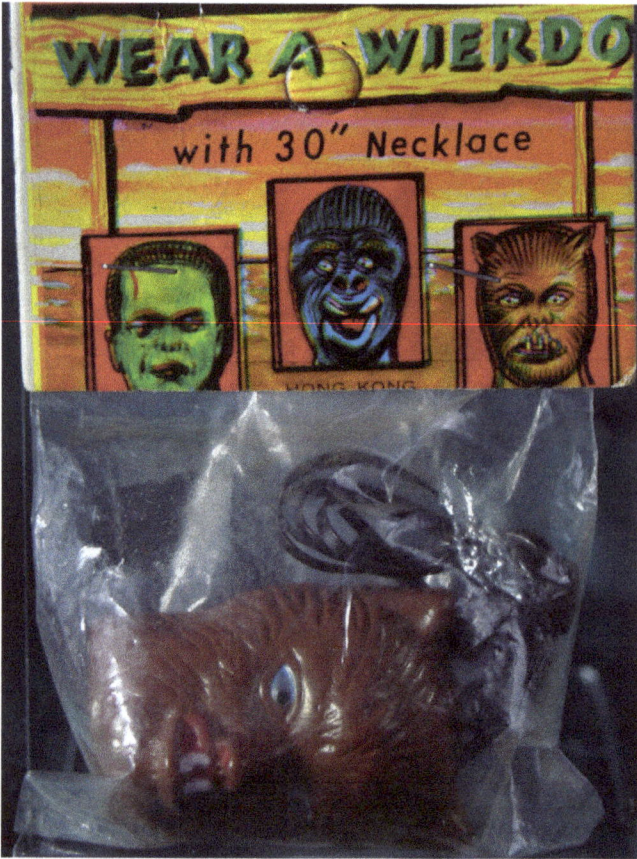

Left:
Wear a Wierdo (sic) necklace of the Wolfman; manufacturer and date unknown.

Below Right:
A Wolfman pencil sharpener by ABG which were produced during the 1960s.

Below Left:
AHI produced Fright Flashers" f Frankenstein and The Wolfman (pictured) in 1981; it was the last monster item the company produced.

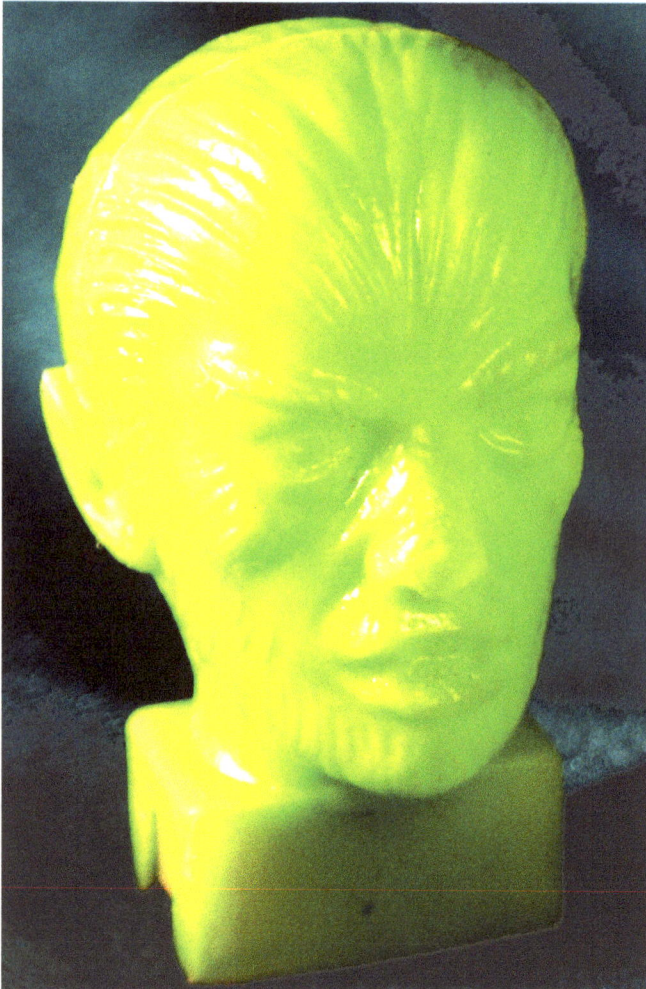

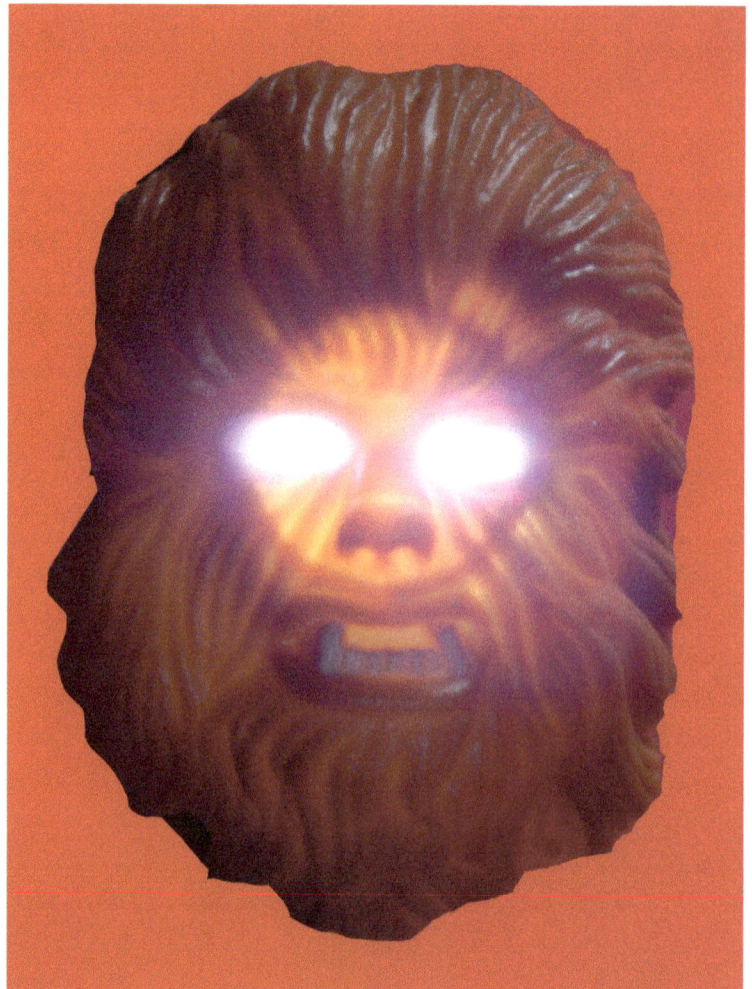

Above:
Imperial Toys capitalized on Jaws with a variety of impulse items such as rings and the logical squirting shark.

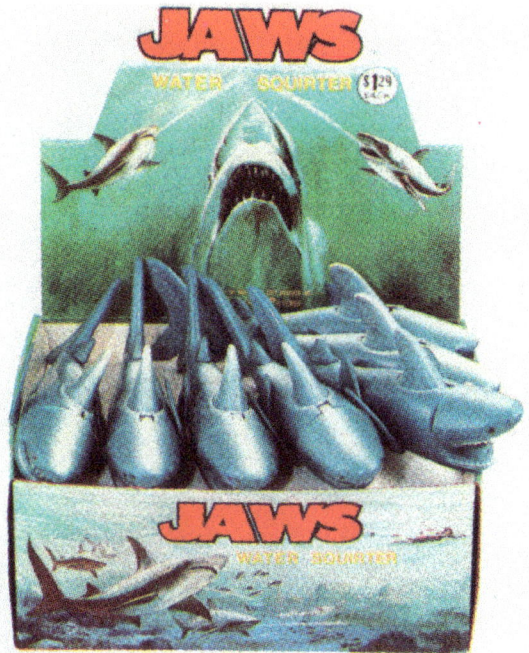

Below:
A rubber shark by Imperial now becomes "official" thanks to a sticker with the Jaws logo.

For Ages 3 and up

FRANKENSTEIN

GLOW PUTTY

Non-Toxic
Non Flowing
Non Sticking

- SHAPES
- STRETCHES
- TRANSFERS
- COMICS

SUPER BOUNCE

To activate glow,
place putty in
sunlight or
near lamp.

Net Weight .47 Oz.
13 grams

GLOWS IN THE DARK

© 1979 LARAMI CORP.

5 x 7   LARAMI CORP., PHILA., PA. 19107   ITEM NO. 8347-7   MADE IN U.S.A.

PRINTED IN HONG KONG   PACKAGED IN USA

Larami introduced Glow Putty featuring generic renditions of Dracula, Frankenstein and the Alien in 1981.

Chapter Three
The Future is Fantastic

To Boldly Go....and make a quick buck.

Children's obsession with Science Fiction properties is nothing new, but it is something that grew considerably in the later half of the 20th century, with the inception of television.

Comic based characters such as Buck Rogers and Flash Gordon have seen many incarnations over the past few decades with a slew of toys following in tow.

Television programs such as Planet of the Apes, Doctor Who, Star Trek and Space:1999 brought the world licensed merchandise booms - long before George Lucas took us to a galaxy far, far away.

The increased interest in Science Fiction properties during the 1970s saw Rack Toy manufacturers attempting to capture the trend in any way possible, creating many memorable and sometimes hilarious items.

Ben Cooper Planet of the Apes Jigglers in their original counter display box from 1974.

Kids Go Ape

Planet of the Apes thrilled moviegoers in 1968, but it wasn't until a network TV airing in 1973 that toy manufacturers saw any potential. The ratings, specifically the number of children that tuned in, caused CBS to order a weekly Apes television series.

In what can only be described as the first succesful movie merchandising blitz, Christmas of 1974 was truly ruled by Apes. Hundreds of different branded items were produced in this short period, including numerous low cost Rack Toys.

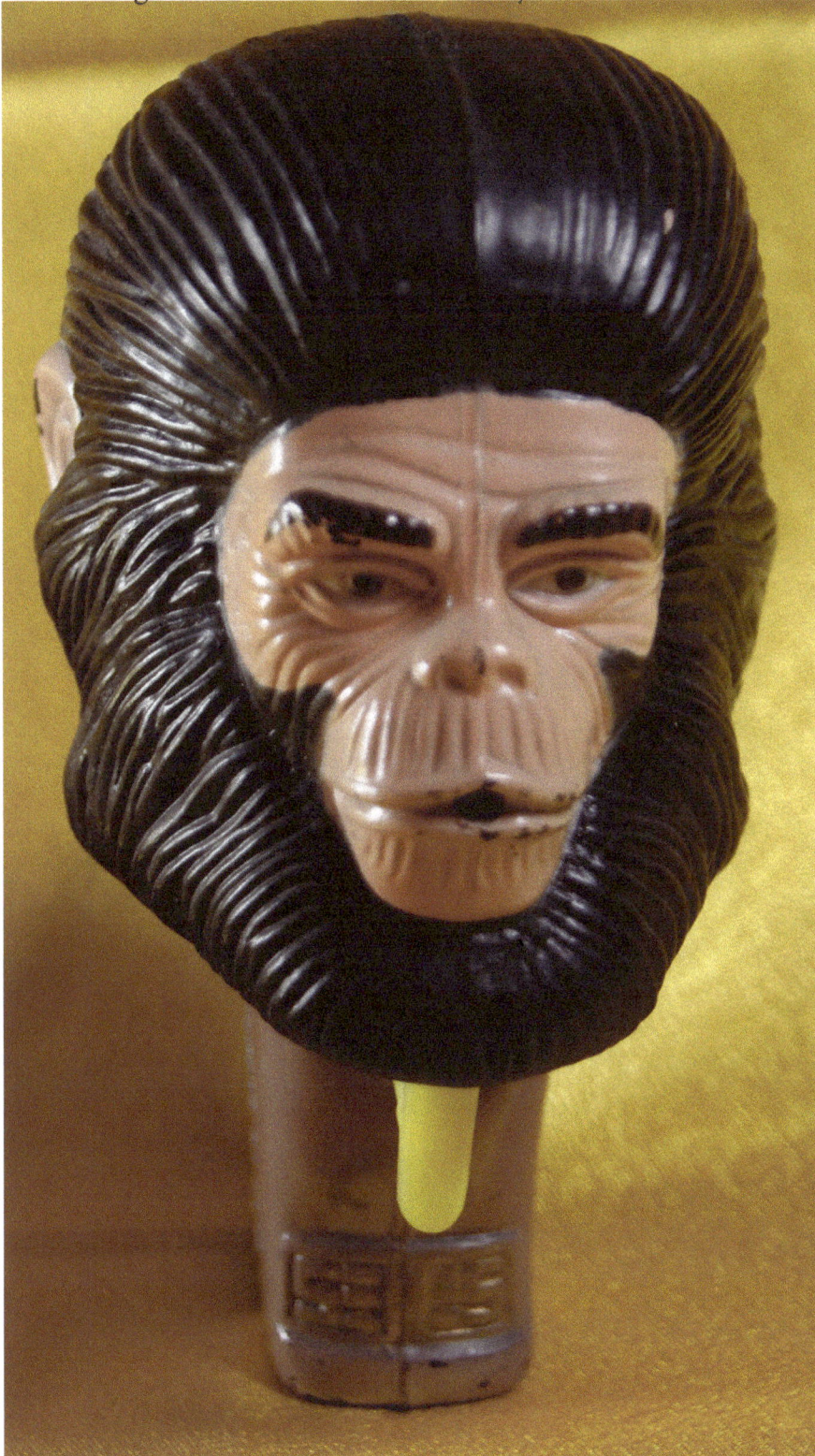

Above:
Planet of the Apes MagicSlate from 1974."
Left:
An AHI Galen Water Gun from 1974.
Below:
A very rare 1974 Planet of the Apes Water Gun display box from the AHI catalog.

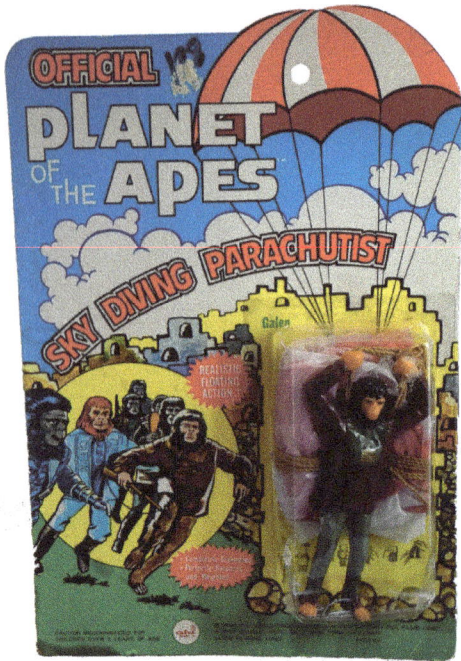

Left:
An early AHI Apes Parachutist figure which originally came without a rifle in 1974.

Above:
A later version of the Parachutist which now come bearing arms. and is the more commonly found variation.

OFFICIAL
PLANET
OF THE APES™
HELICOPTER

SOARS **HIGH**
IN THE AIR

TO LAUNCH
PULL STRING ON
AUTOMATIC
REWINDING MOTOR

ahi

*AHI produced many Ape toys by retooling items made for Batman, like this Helicopter
which comes complete with Ape Soldier pilot and lack of continuity to the film or
television series.*

Another retooled AHI Batman item, this
1974 Stunt Cycle now had Cornelius popping
wheelies in your driveway.

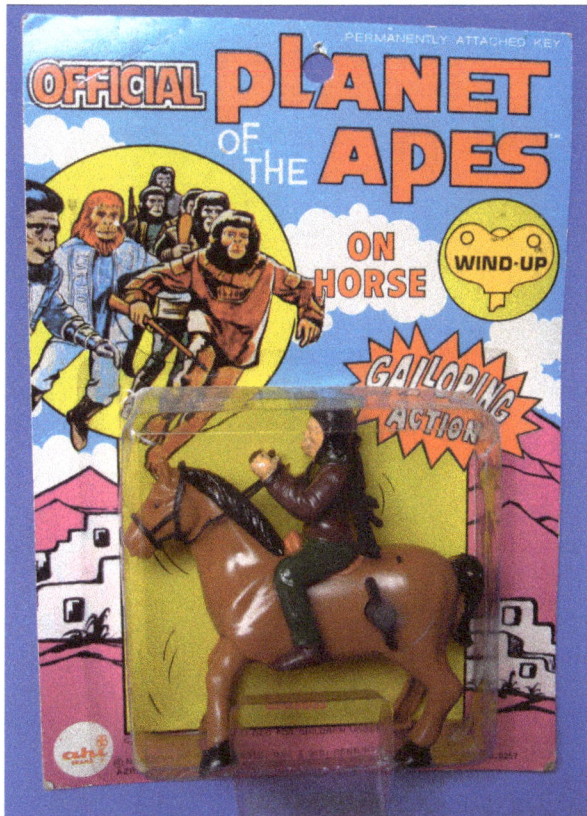

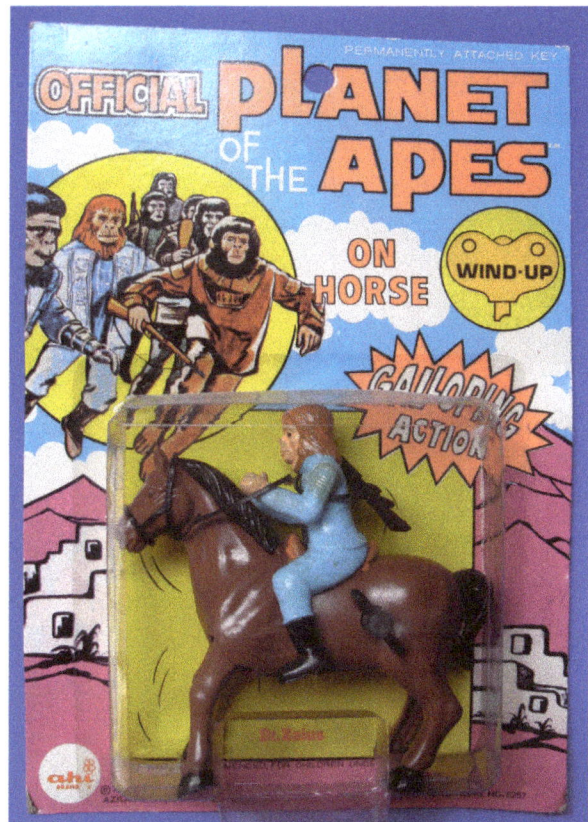

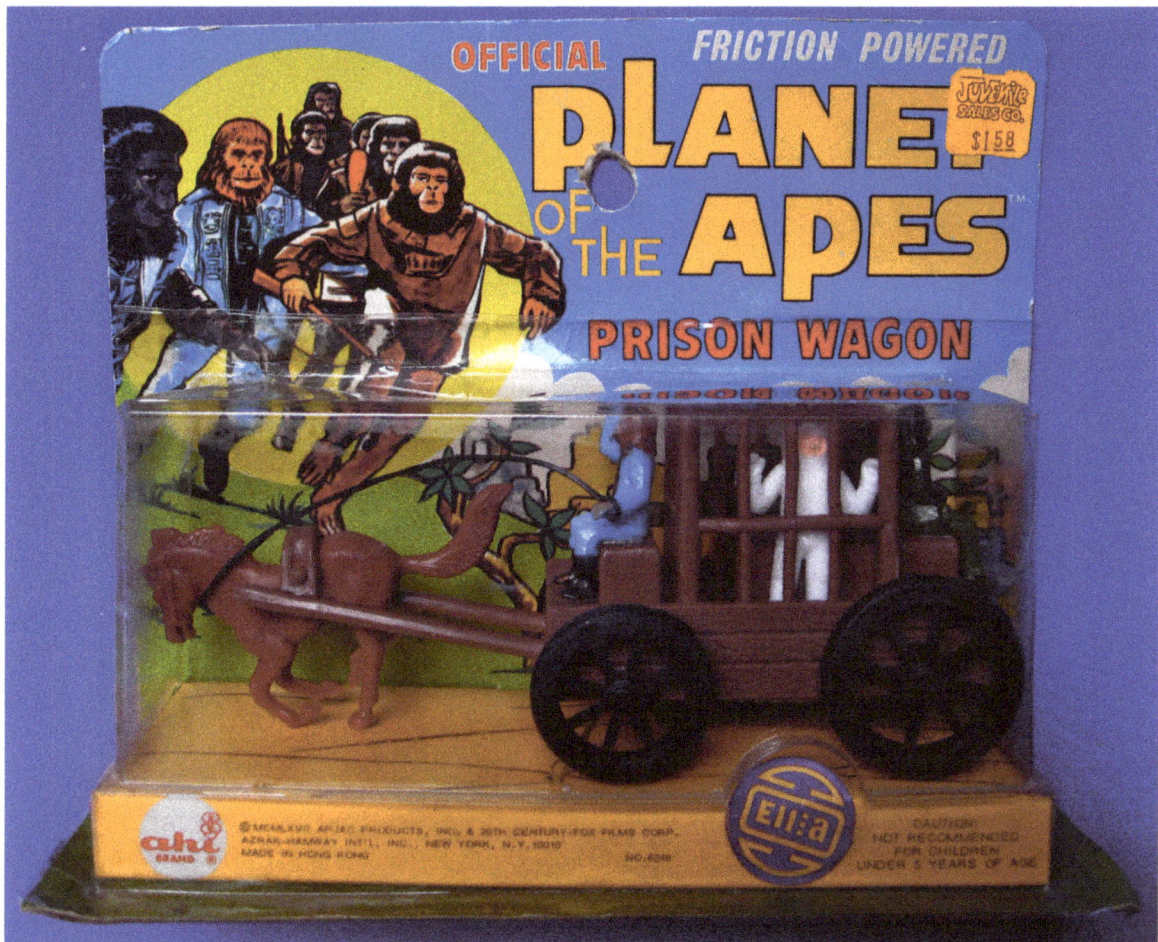

A 1974 trio of AHI Planet of the Apes Wind Ups and Friction Vehicles that remain very collectible to this

Highly Illogical...Highly Profitable

Like "Apes" Star Trek's merchandise bonanza didn't come until years after its inception. Cancelled after three seasons on network TV, the show thrived in syndication, captivating a younger audience.

By 1976, Star Trek mania ran wild with the brand being used to sell everything from socks to metal detectors.

Rack Toy manufacturers capitalized on both the original series and the subsequent motion picture producing low cost quick fixes for Trekkies in need.

Above:
Larami binoculars were produced in 1968, while the series was still on network television, hence the mention of NBC on the package.

#9238 Star Trek Flashlite Ray Gun. Pistol-shaped flashlight with Star Trek emblem. Comes with two genuine Eveready batteries. Card size: 7½" x 10¾".

#9239 Star Trek Binoculars. Only officially-licensed binoculars with all the appeal of one of TV's top shows. Powerful, full-sized, adjustable. With strap. Card size: 7½" x 10¾".

Left:
A snippet from the 1969 Larami Toys catalog showing the first Star Trek Rack Toys produced.

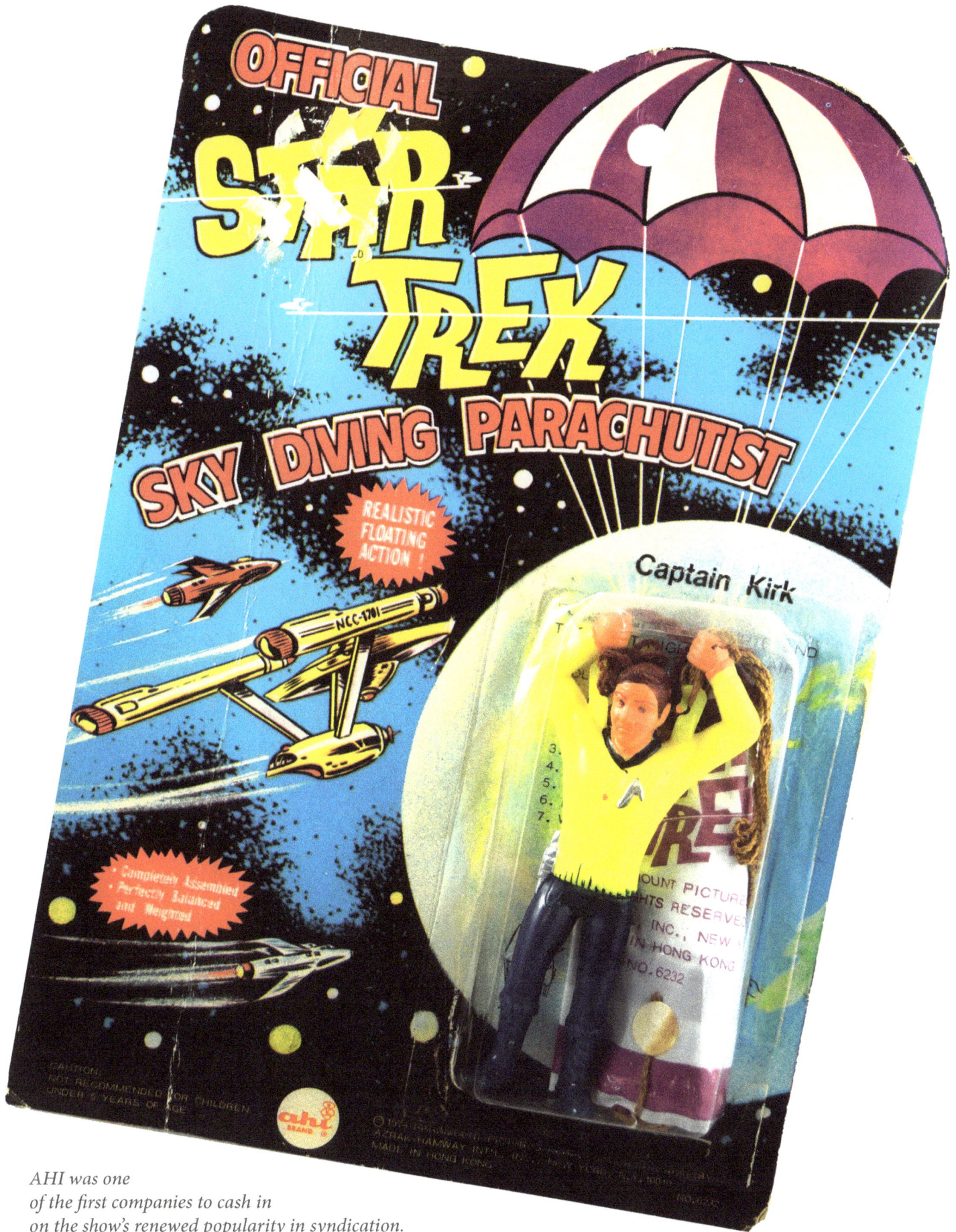

OFFICIAL **STAR TREK**
SKY DIVING PARACHUTIST

REALISTIC FLOATING ACTION!

NCC-1701

Completely Assembled
Perfectly Balanced and Weighted

Captain Kirk

AHI was one
of the first companies to cash in
on the show's renewed popularity in syndication.
This Kirk parachutist figure was a popular item in 1975.

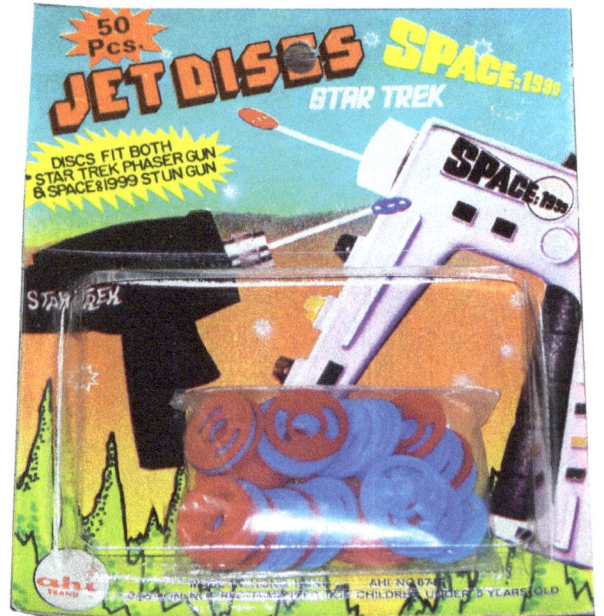

Clockwise from the Top:

AHI Phaser Ray Gun from 1975 doubled as a flash light.

The Enterprise itself was a star of the show, as evidenced by this innovative 1975 AHI water gun.

AHI sold replacement jet disks for Remco (a company owned by AHI) toy pistols. This rare 1976 item shows cross promotion with Space:1999.

AHI Phaser Saucer Gun from 1975.

The Flying Enterprise by AHI was a best selling item and looks like a lot of fun.

Star Trek Pinball by AHI in 1975 came in two flavors: Kirk or Spock.

NEW TRANSFER SOLUTION

CAUTION: NOT RECOMMENDED FOR CHILDREN UNDER 3 YEARS OF AGE

STAR TREK

THE MOTION PICTURE PUTTY

Non Toxic • Non Flowing • Non Sticking

TRANSFERS PUTTY IMAGE TO ANY SURFACE

As seen on TV

Copyright © 1979 Paramount Pictures Corporation. All Rights Reserved. TM Designates a Trademark of Paramount Pictures Corporation. Manufactured by LARAMI CORP., Phila., Pa. 19107 Under Exclusive License From Paramount Pictures Corporation. The Trademark Owner.

LARAMI

5 x 7   ITEM NO. 8348-5

CAUTION: NOT RECOMMENDED FOR CHILDREN UNDER 3 YEARS OF AGE

STAR TREK

THE MOTION PICTURE

I.D. SET

THE FEDERATION

CAPTAIN

LARAMI

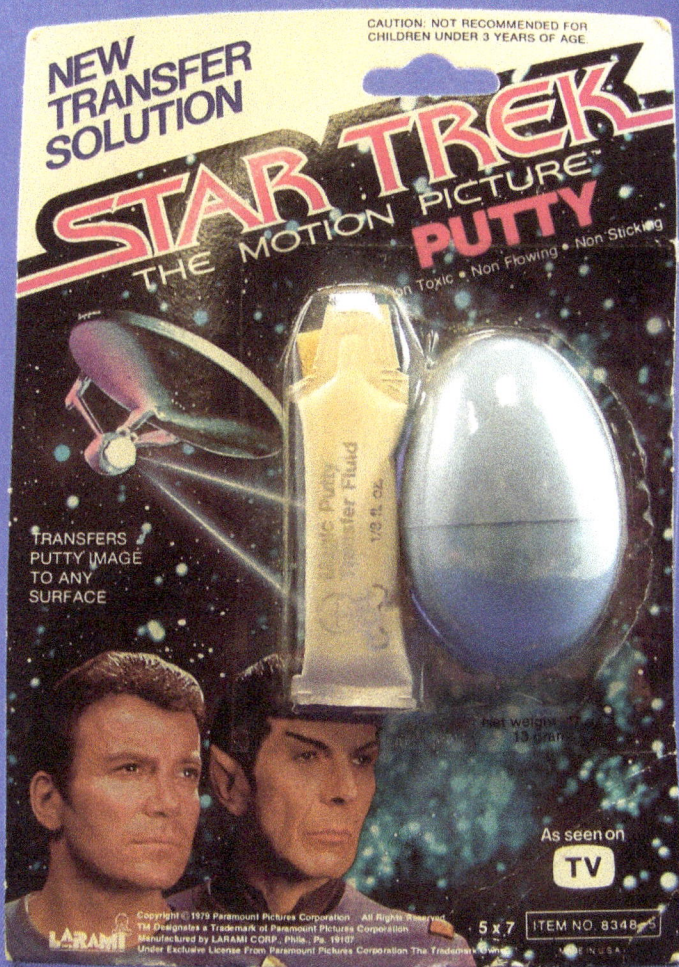

No. 8039-0
STAR TREK
PHOTON BLASTER
PK: 2 doz./12 doz./4.00'
Card Size: 6" x 9"

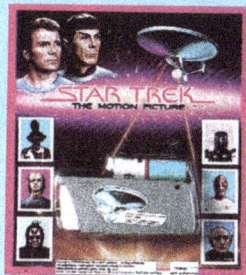

No. 8048-1
STAR TREK
FLASHLITE
PK: 2 doz./24 doz./2.72'
Card Size: 6" x 7"

No. 8053-1
STAR TREK
SPACE VIEWER
PK: 2 doz./24 doz./5.75'
Card Size: 6" x 9"

No. 8055-6
STAR TREK
GIANT PUZZLES
PK: 3 doz./36 doz./6.50'
Card Size: 6" x 10"

No. 8063-0
STAR TREK
SIGNAL GUN
PK: 2 doz./12 doz./5.42'
Card Size: 6" x 10"

Star Trek: the Motion Picture saw many licensors, such as Larami beaming aboard, hoping to recapture the sales heat the original series delivered.

Sadly, the film wasn't as friendly to children's imaginations and the majority of its merchandise languished on store shelves.

Clockwise from the Top:
An array of largely uninspired Motion Picture items from Larami in 1980.

To the Moon!

"Space:1999" was a syndicated, high budget series produced in 1975 as a response to the massive popularity that "Star Trek" reruns were enjoying.

Hoping that lightning would strike twice, hundreds of toy manufacturers signed up before the first episode hit the airwaves.

Most prolific among them was Azrak Hamway, who produced a slew of merchandise based on the success model they had going with "Star Trek".

While the series failed to be a phenomenon, the resulting merchandising is not only memorable, but quite collectible among fans.

Above:
An Eagle Transporter by AHI, these sleek vehicles proved to be the stars of the show.

Below:
A lower cost die-cast version of the Eagle produced by Yot Toys , a UK based manufacturer.

Above:
A 1975 Space:1999 Moon Car from AHI, a fairly accurate depiction of the buggies seen on the series.

Above Right:
Larami's 1976 Galaxy Time Meter is simply a wrist watch with the series logo slapped on it.

Right:
This Marx Communicator is a very sought after item, but it didn't resemble the actual hardware from the show.

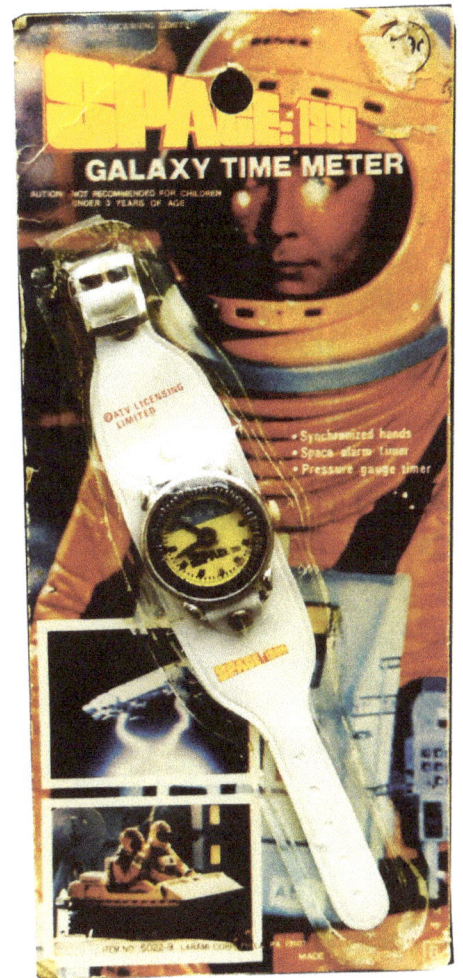

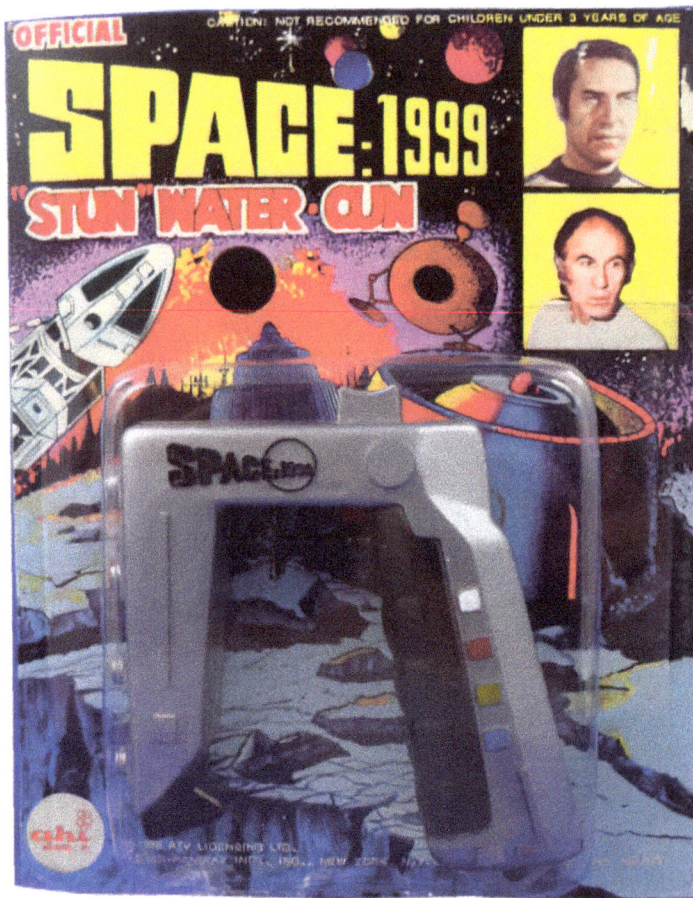

Above Left:
The Eagle Water Gun was a fun piece captilizing on the popularity of the vehicles. This one is in yellow "test plastic" meaning even early production sample items were sold off to stores.

Above Right:
A surprisingly accurate replica of the Stun Gun as a AHI Water Gun.

Right:
The original hand drawn card artwork, photo from the AHI archives.

For Ages 3 and up

RAY BRADBURY'S

THE MARTIAN CHRONICLES

FIGURE

- FULLY POSEABLE
- COLLECT ALL THE MARTIAN CHRONICLES FIGURES

CHARLES FRIES PRODUCTIONS INC. ALL RIGHTS RESERVED

8½ 9½   LARAMI CORP., PHILA., PA. 19107   ITEM NO. 3050-2   MADE IN HONG KONG

During the 1970s Sci-Fi craze, even a TV mini series could see merchandise. Based on the classic Ray Bradbury novel, The Martian Chronicles was licensed by Larami for a series of somewhat poorly made action figures. By choosing not to produce any of the human characters, Larami ruined our first, best hope for a Rock Hudson action figure.

CAUTION: NOT RECOMMENDED FOR CHILDREN UNDER 3 YEARS OF AGE.

BattlestaR GALACTICA

*A trademark of and licensed by © 1978 Universal City Studios, Inc. All rights reserved.

GALACTIC CRUISER

- DIE CAST METAL
- NON TOXIC PAINT
- STURDY CONSTRUCTION
- FREE ROLLING

6 x 7   LARAMI CORP., PHILA., PA. 19107   ITEM NO. 8425-1   MADE IN HONG KONG

CAUTION: NOT RECOMMENDED FOR CHILDREN UNDER 3 YEARS OF AGE.

BattlestaR GALACTICA

L.E.M. LANDER

CAUTION: NOT RECOMMENDED FOR CHILDREN UNDER 3 YEARS OF AGE.

BattlestaR GALACTICA

SOLAR EXPLORER
- HIGH POWERED LENS
- 2 SECTION TELESCOPE
- ADJUSTABLE BINOCULARS WITH CARRYING STRAP

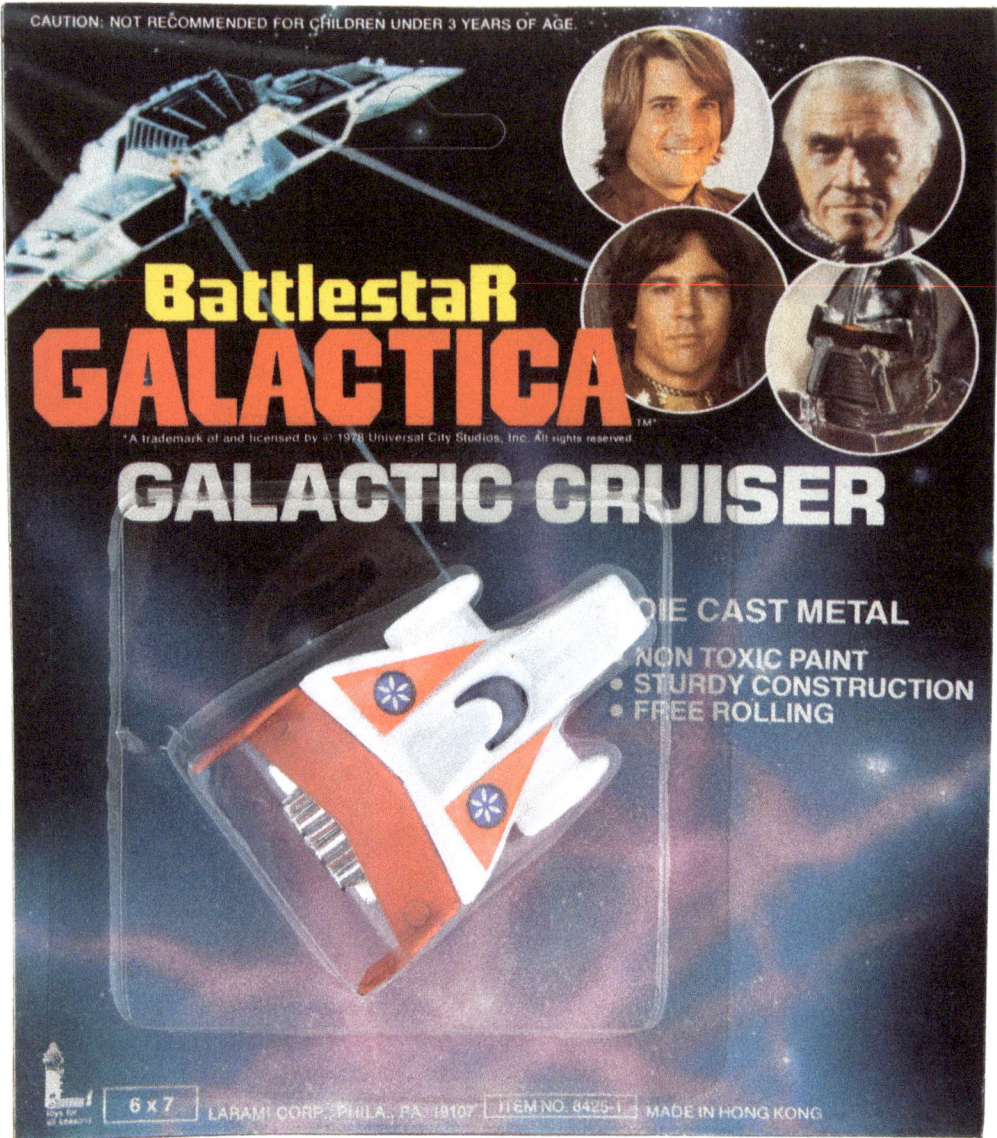

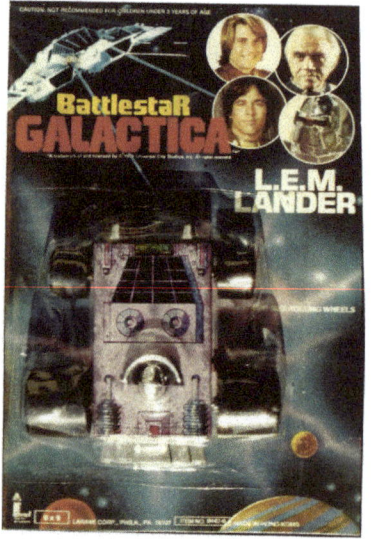

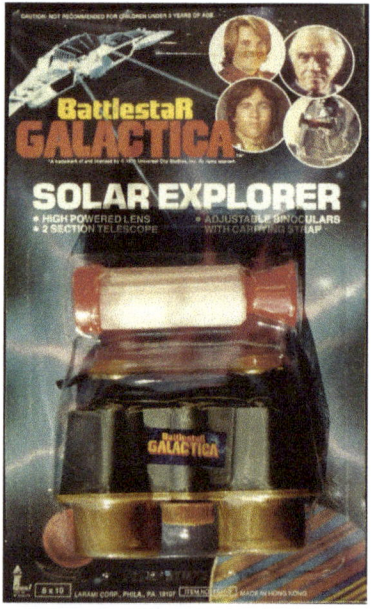

Clockwise from the top:

A variety of completely uninspired items based on "Battlestar Galactica". The Galactic Cruiser was sold under many licenses as were L.E.M Lander, the Solar Expolorer and Watch Set.

The "Cylon" Sunglasses were later sold as Star Trek:The Motion Picture Sunglasses.

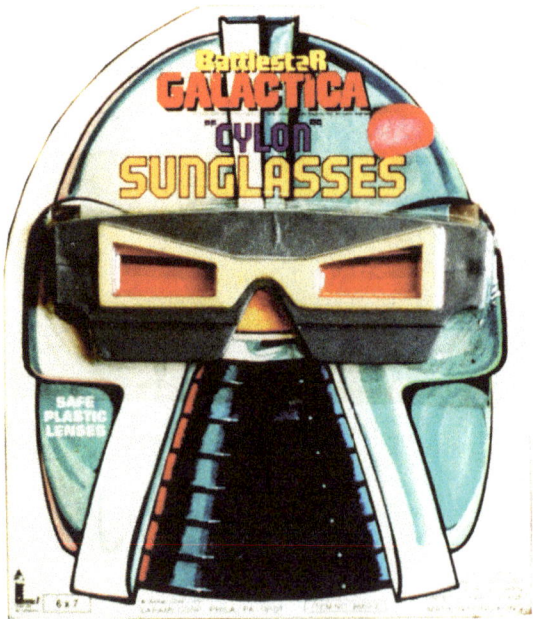

BattlestaR GALACTICA CYLON SUNGLASSES

SAFE PLASTIC LENSES

CAUTION: NOT RECOMMENDED FOR CHILDREN UNDER 3 YEARS OF AGE.

BattlestaR GALACTICA

WATCH SET

Buck Rogers in the 25th Century wasn't going to win any awards for quality in Science Fiction, but the tongue in cheek series was a good deal of fun and attracted a large fan base of children.

Buck was also a merchandising sensation with numerous Rack Toy companies courting the show during its two year run.

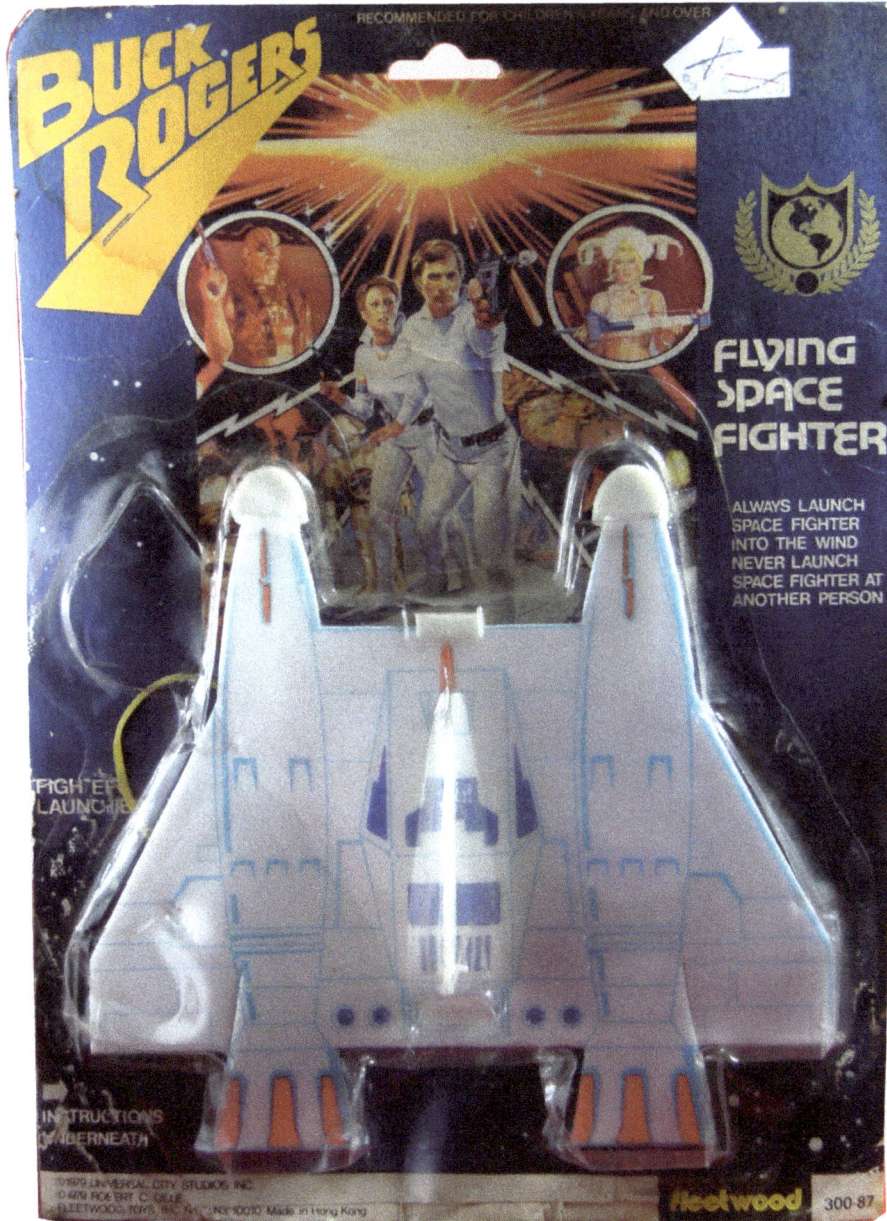

Above:
1980 Buck Rogers Space Marbles by Imperial Toy.

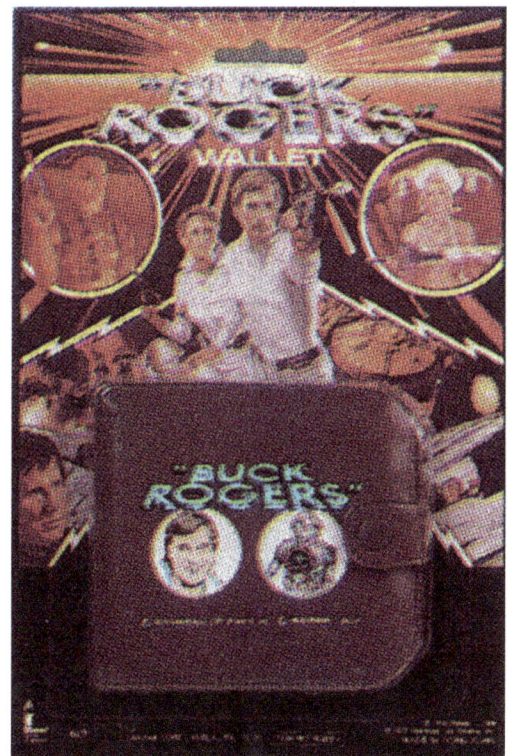

Above:
Fleetwood Toys produced a number of show accurate Buck Rack Toys such as this Flying Space Fighter.

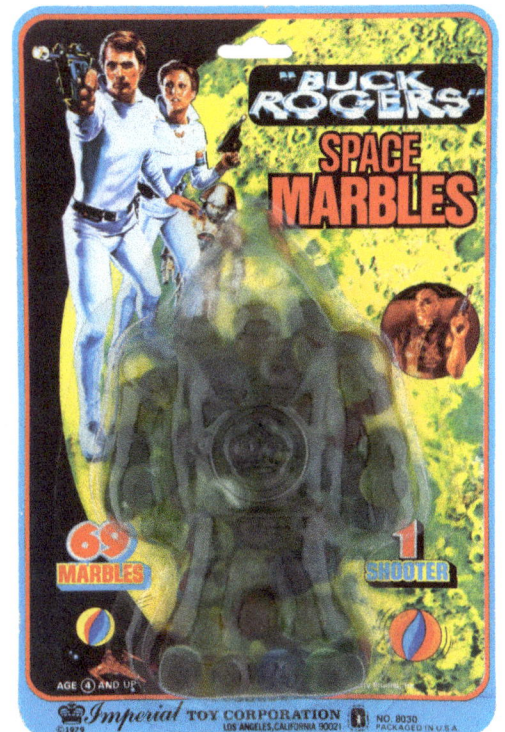

Above:
Larami gave the world the Buck Rogers Wallet in 1980.

Above:
Flash Gordon Tootsie Toy Star Ships.

Right:
Flash Gordon was the original Science Fiction superhero so it's no surprise merchandise was still around in the 1970s, as evidenced by this printing set produced by MSS.

Opposite:
A Flash Gordon Space Glider also produced by MSS.

Steven Spielberg's "Close Encounters of the Third Kind" generated more critical praise than Star Wars did, but not the merchandise. Imperial Toys made these Extra Terrestrial figures which sold slowly at retail; probably because few children wanted a figure that looked like a naked octagenarian.

Chapter Four
TV and Movie Super Stars

Hollywood Magic

Television programs, particularly one hour dramas and situation comedies, rarely see much success in toy stores. The biggest reasoning for this is the gamble involved with new properties. If a show gets cancelled, it could spell financial doom for a company.

The risk can be even greater for film, where a movie can come and go in a weekend.

The opposite, however, is true for Rack Toys, because many of these toys were simply re-packed and re-labelled versions of existing items. A relatively low investment was needed to produce new products. This encouraged manufacturers to take risks when looking for new properties.

By adding the face of Kojak to a cap gun for example, the Rack Toy manufacturer can get higher recognition and increased sales.

This practice is so common that Rack Toys are sometimes the only merchandise a television show or movie ever sees. Many "One Season Wonders" and "Box Office Bombs" were courted by Rack Toy manufacturers leaving behind a series of strange and nonsensical merchandise for future generations.

Above: *The smiling cast of Police Woman adorn this 1974 Crime Lab by MSS.*
Left: *Mod Squad Jr. Water Guns by Larami 1972.*

君も僕も諜報員です

きみ ぼく ちょうほういん

★★★★

アンクル 通信ライト

007 ジェムス ボンド

KP

This flashlight from Japan covers all bases by using not one but four TV and movie licenses. Clockwise from the top left The Man from U.N.C.L.E., James Bond, Gappa and The Space Giants. It's the coolest movie never made. There is no date on this but I'd bet money it's from 1966.

The serio-comic adventures of the 4077 M*A*S*H saw a small amount of AHI toys like this helicopter from 1974.

Left:

The serious medical drama of M*A*S*H spin off series, Trapper John M.D. wasn't the talk of the playground. However, it didn't stop Ja-Ru from capitalizing on it's name in 1980.

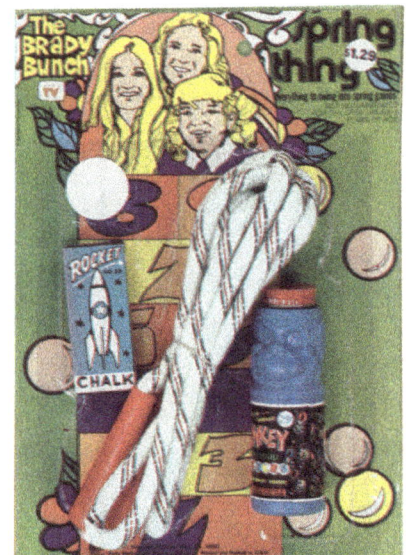

Above

The popularity of the Brady Bunch in syndication meant that Larami could continue selling merchandise well past the series cancellation. These Boy and Girl toy sets are from the 1976 Catalog.

Watching the Detectives

TV Crime dramas may not have been habitually watched by young children but their recognition factor by both kids and adults helped elevate items such as cap guns and walkie talkies above generic versions.

Right:
Jak Pak toys believed the image of Matt Houston star Lee Horsely would motivate kids to buy in 1985. They should have used series co-star Pamela Hensley.

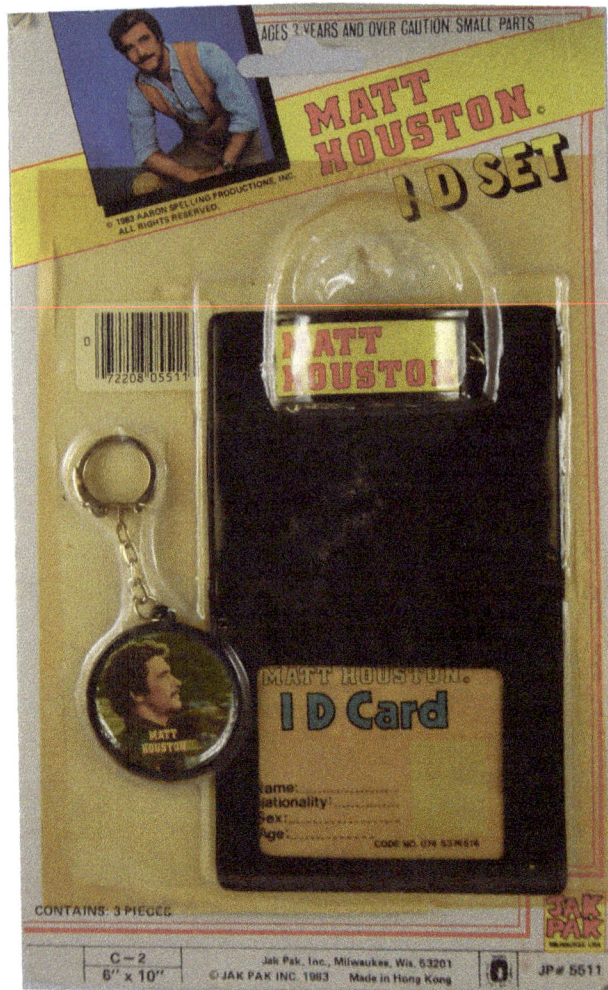

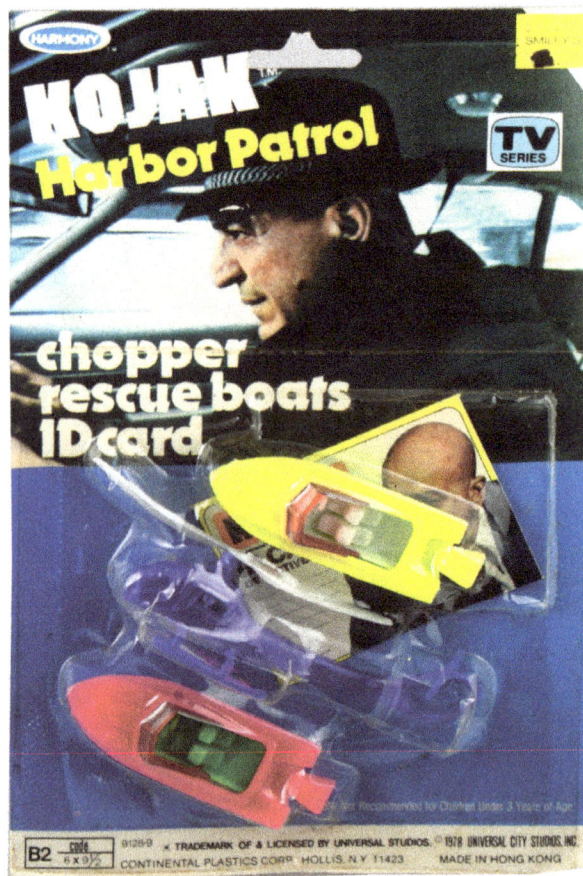

Above:
Gordy Toys Simon & Simon Walkie Talkies from 1981.

Right:
A 1974 set of boats somehow based on Kojak by Harmony.

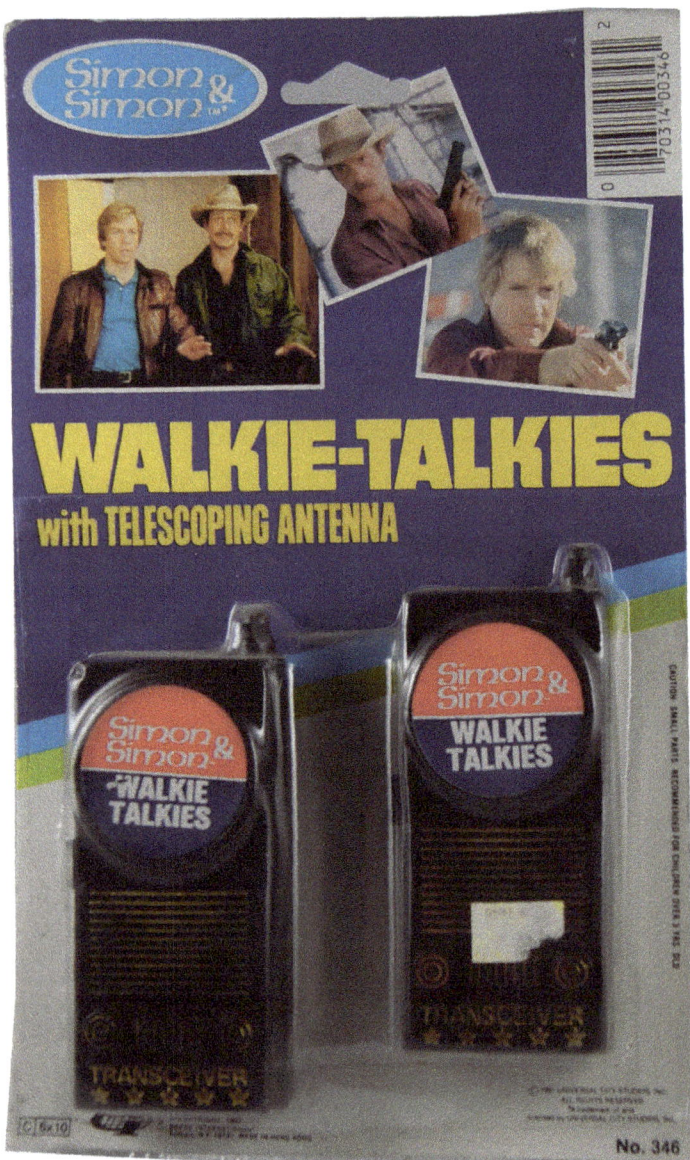

*Gordy Toys put the Dukes of Hazzard logo on absolutely everything they could in 1981.
Items like handcuffs and ray guns sold well thanks to a ravenous fan base of children.*

Above:

The movie version of Annie created a licensing boom that sadly did not have a happy ending. Gordy created a slew of low cost items in 1982.

Above Right:

The Laverne and Shirley Secratary Set from Harmony features a strange tiny book case and a completely anachronistic pocket calculator.

Right:

Some "Pearl" Rings for the ladies also from Harmony in 1975.

Left:

The popularity of NBC's "CHiPs" translated well into toy sales as the majority of the viewers were children.

Below:

The vehicles were as popular as the actors, and Fleetwood Toys captilized on that during the series run. This is a catalog shot from 1982.

300-17

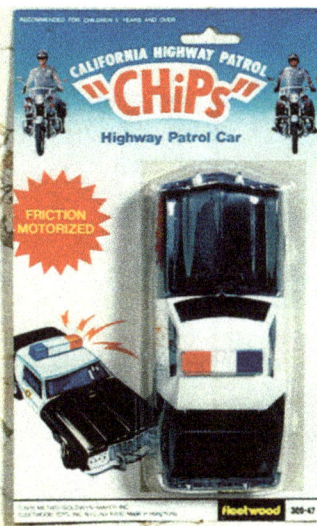

300-47

300-80

Left:

The light hearted antics of the Love Boat shouldn't have lent itself to as much merchandise as it did. This Barber Shop set by Fleetwood Toys exemplifies the amount of thought and care that went into many of the items.

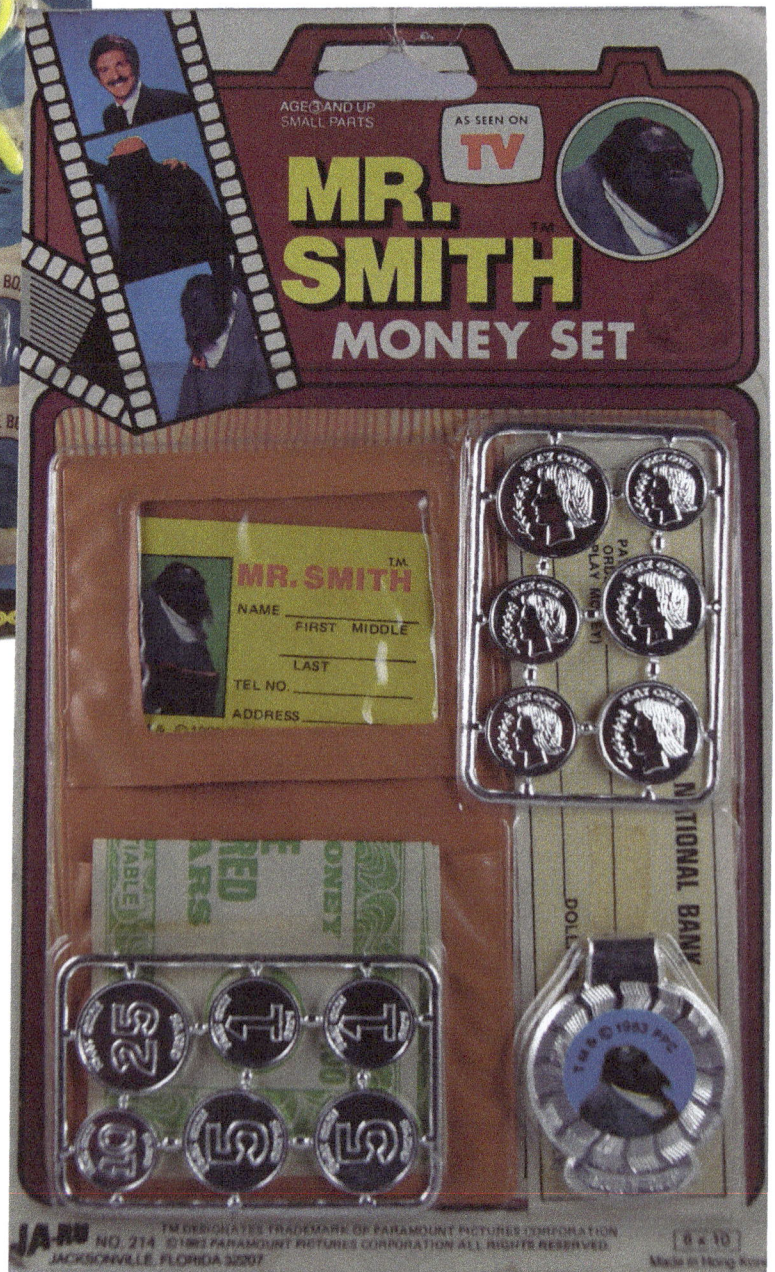

Right:

Mr. Smith was a 1983 NBC sitcom about a talking orangutan that worked in Washington (I'm not making this up). It was quickly cancelled and this Money Set by Ja-Ru is one of the few items that prove it existed.

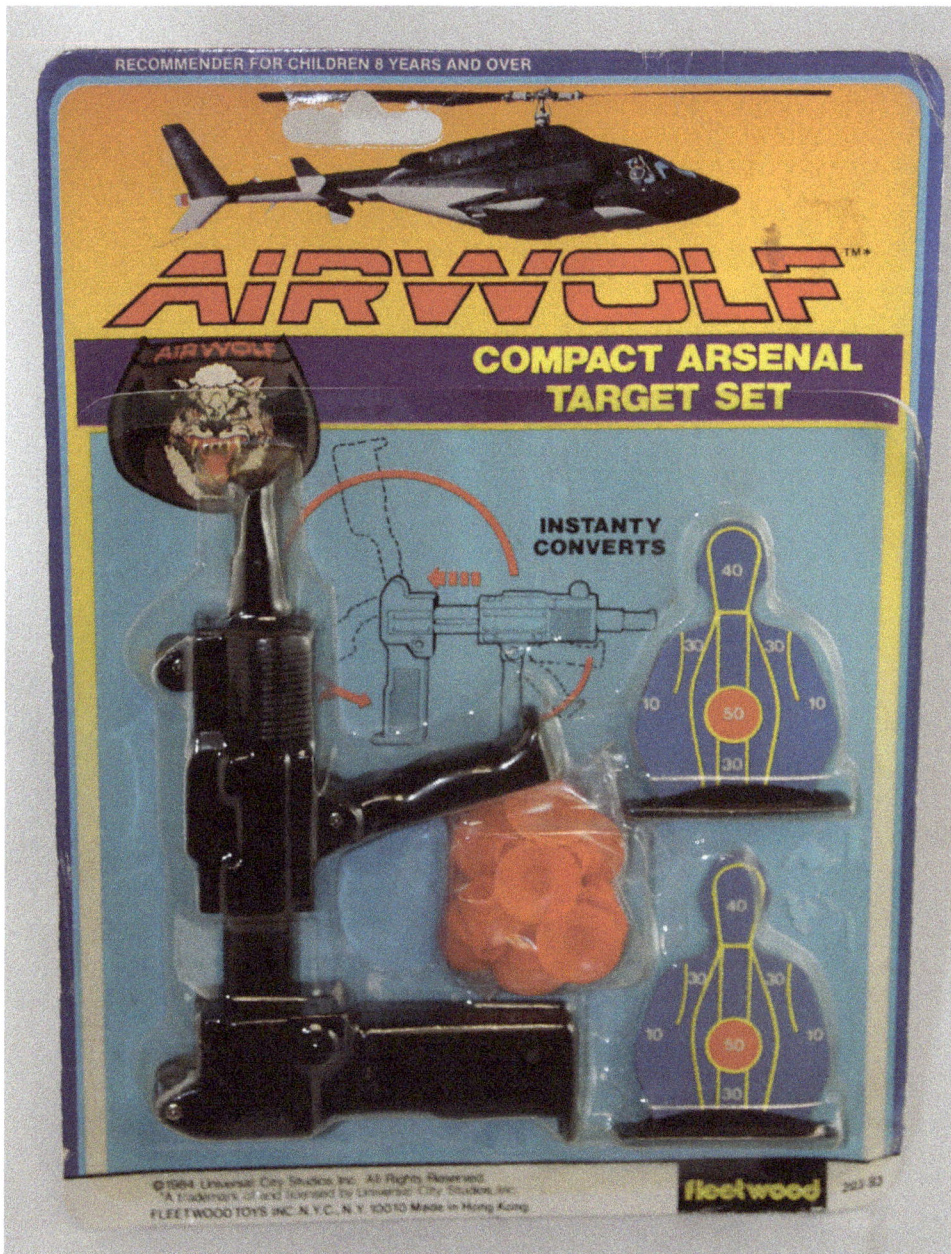

AIRWOLF™*

COMPACT ARSENAL TARGET SET

INSTANTY CONVERTS

40
30   30
10   [50]   10
30

40
30   30
10   [50]   10
30

©1984 Universal City Studios Inc. All Rights Reserved.
*A trademark of and licensed by Universal City Studios, Inc.
FLEETWOOD TOYS INC. N.Y.C. N.Y. 10010 Made in Hong Kong.

fleetwood   293-53

Left:
Airwolf's adult themes kept it off regular toy shelves, but Fleetwood Toys capitilized on the name. This Compact Arsenal Target set was one of many Airwolf based toys they released in 1984.

Right:
Fleetwood Toys snapped up the rights to the short lived series BJ and the Bear. It is not known how much of the merchandise made it to market. This image is from the 1982 Fleetwood Toys catalog.

RECOMMENDED FOR CHILDREN 5 YEARS AND OVER

BJ AND THE BEAR™

As seen on TV

Scale Model of KENWORTH™ AERODYNE with Trailer

300-02

300-02

RECOMMENDED FOR CHILDREN OVER 3 YEARS

STREET HAWK ™*

Walkie Talkie

STREET HAWK

STREET HAWK

INSTRUCTIONS ON BACK

FLEETWOOD TOYS INC. N.Y.C., N.Y. 10010 Made in Hong Kong.   fleetwood   203-6

Left:

Street Hawk was mid season replacement that only ran 13 episodes in 1985. Its cancellation forced companies such as Kenner to put their toy lines on hold. However Fleetwood Toys already had Street Hawk merchandise on the pegs as evidenced by this Walkie Talkie set.

Below:

Manimal only lasted half a season on NBC in 1984. These strange action figures, some of which were also sold under The Sword and the Sorcerer banner, may be the only toy tie-ins the show received.

Left:
The TV sensation The A-Team created a flurry of merchandise by Fleetwood Toys in 1984.

Below:
The star of the A-Team, Mr T. had such popularity during this period that he could merchandise his own persona, as evidenced by this 1984 Imperial Toy Jewelry set.

Right:

This Knight Rider Whistle was just one of the many items that Larami produced in 1984 for the hit series.

Below Left:

1984 Knight Rider stickers by Diamond Toy Makers.

Below Right:

Baywatch Water Rescue Set by Ja-Ru in 1991 seems to suggest that the show was watched by more than teenage boys.

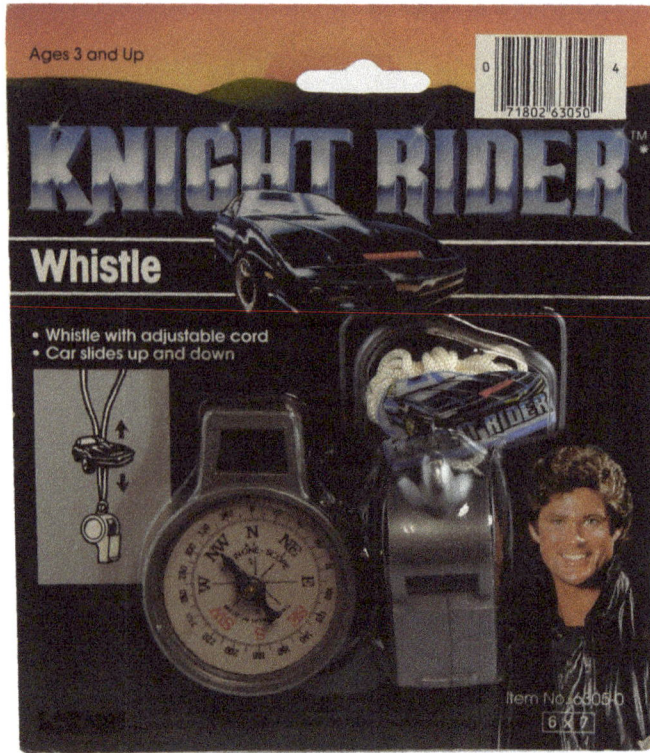

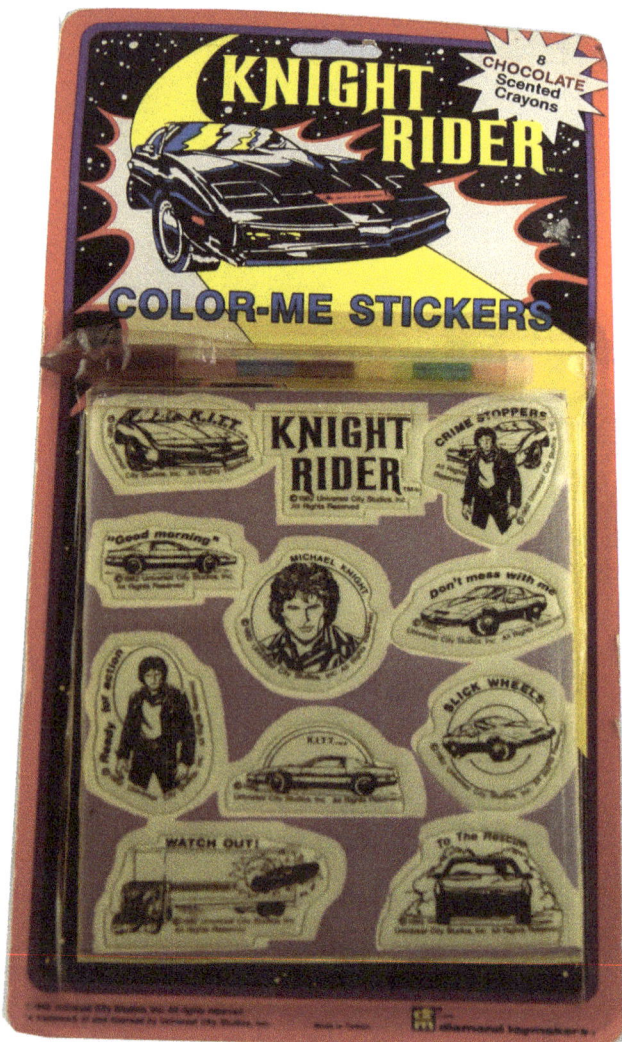

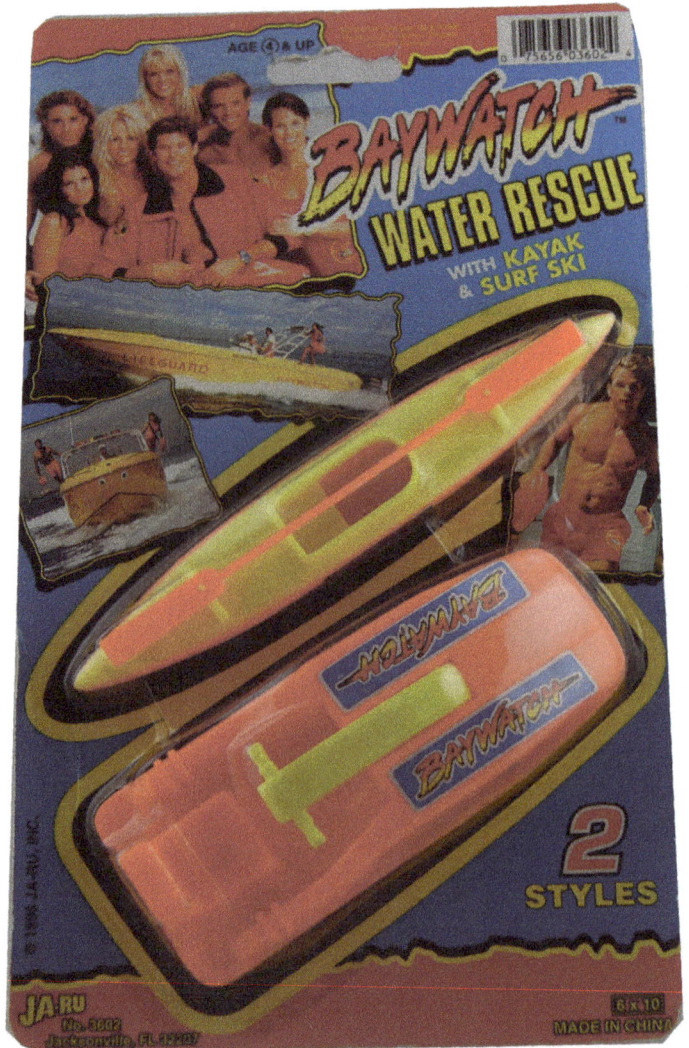

Knight Rider

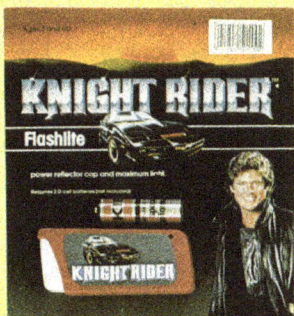

FLASHLITE
#6308-0
Card Size 6 x 7

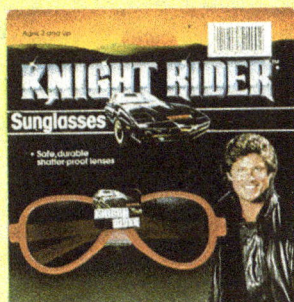

SUNGLASSES
#6303-0
Card Size 6 x 7

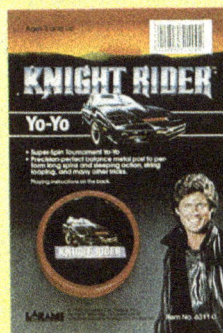

BUTTERFLY YO-YO
#6311-0
Card Size 5 x 7½

HANDCUFFS
#6306-0
Card Size 6 x 9

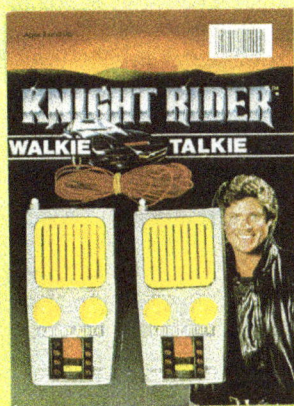

WALKIE-TALKIE
#6313-0
Card Size 6 x 9

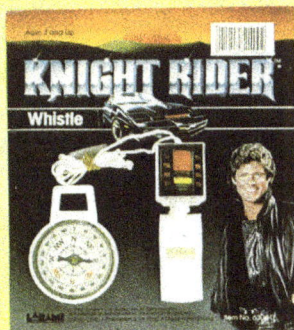

WHISTLE & COMPASS
#6305-0
Card Size 6 x 7

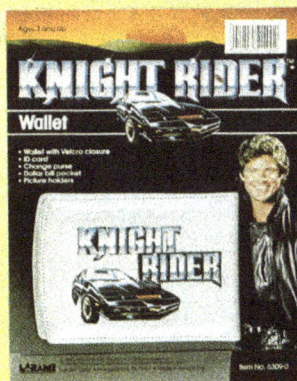

WALLET
#6309-0
Card Size 6¾ x 8½

SELF-INKING STAMP SET
#6312-0
Card Size 6 x 7

VISOR GLASSES
#6302-0
Card Size 6½ x 9

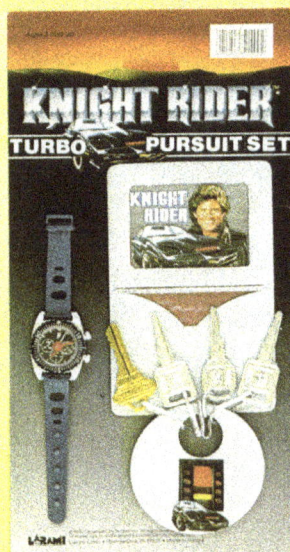

TURBO PURSUIT SET
#6314-0
Card Size 6½ x 12

TIC-TIC WATCH
#6310-0
Card Size 6 x 10

**MICRO CHIP SONIC
WRIST COMMUNICATOR**
#6301-0
Card Size 6 x 12

A whole lot of the Haf from Larami toys 1986 catalog

103

Above:

The now forgotten 1986 action film The Patriot spawned an action figure series by Fleetwood Toys.

Left:

Steven Spielberg's unsuccesful film 1941 spawned little merchandise, save for a handful of items produced by Imperial Toy Corporation in 1979. The figure on the bottom bears the likeness of John Belushi.

Fleetwood Toys Karate Kid Drum and Headband probably got some kids beaten up in 1985.

MICHAEL DUDIKOFF AS JOE

AMERICAN NINJA™

The deadliest art of the Orient is now in the hands of an American.

SAFETY STAR DART

ALL ONE PIECE

CANNOT PULL APART

RECOMMENDED FOR CHILDREN OVER 5 YEARS

DARTS NUMCHUCK SET

fleetwood

© CANNON FILMS INC
and CANNON INTERNATIONAL B.V.
LIC. BY CANNON FILMS INC

TOY INC
NEW YORK N.Y. 10018
MADE IN HONG KONG

400-07

Left:

The kid who used this 1985 American Ninja set from Fleetwood probably fared better than the one wearing the Karate Kid headband.

Below:

Jak-Pak took some real liberties when exploiting the Rocky movie series in 1986, that is unless the image of Sylvester Stallone immediately conjures thoughts of bubble fun for you.

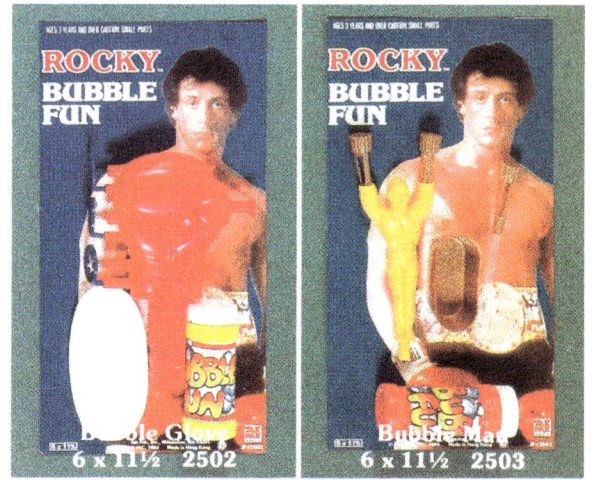

ROCKY BUBBLE FUN

Bubble Glove
6 x 11½ 2502

ROCKY BUBBLE FUN

Bubble Man
6 x 11½ 2503

Right:

Imperial Toys used the image of Chuck Norris to sell The Delta Force toys in 1986. A nation of children purchased them fearing a vicious roundhouse kick if they didn't.

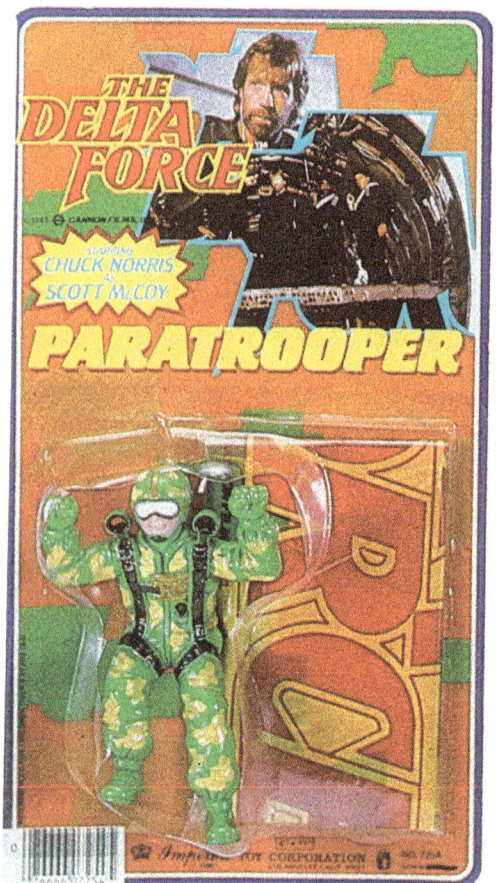

THE DELTA FORCE

STARRING CHUCK NORRIS as SCOTT McCOY

PARATROOPER

the LONE RANGER

HAND PAINTED ACTION FIGURES

© 1981 LONE RANGER TELEVISION INC.
FLEETWOOD TOYS, INC N.Y.C. N.Y. 10010 Made in Hong Kong

fleetwood   300-08

The big screen revival of the Lone Ranger saw Fleetwood saddle up and make some toys in 1980.
The toys fared better than the film, which fizzled at the box office.

The Sword and the Sorcerer may have been an R rated film, but the prevalence of home video and cable in the early 80s meant kids had probably seen it. Fleetwood Toys sold a series of toys based on it in 1983.

"I'd Never Lend My Name to an Inferior Product" -Bart Simpson

The prime time animated antics of the Simpsons had toy manufacturers have a cow when the show first aired. Among them were companies such as Florida's Ja-Ru, who slapped Springfield's favorite family on everything they could think of in 1991.

Chapter Five
Saturday Morning Fun

The Cartoon Conundrum

Thanks to stringent children and advertising Laws pertaining to children, many Saturday morning programs had to differentiate themselves from toy makers. In fact, the FCC ruled that a 1970 Saturday morning series based on the Hot Wheels toy line was in itself a thirty minute commercial.

This Law didn't seem to apply to Rack Toys manufacturers, who grabbed just about every Saturday morning program for their instant recognition factor. Many of toys are now highly collectible and sought after by fans,

In the early 1980s, the ruling on children's advertising was retooled, allowing toy companies to create 30 minute commercials. While this was a boon for many, but didn't change the daily business of a Rack Toy manufacturer.

THE MIGHTY

25¢

HERCULES

MAGIC RING

JUST LIKE
THE MIGHTY HERCULES
OWN RING

- GLOWS IN DARK
- SECRET COMPARTMENT

SAFE • HARMLESS
EXPOSE TO LIGHT
FOR GLOW ACTION
©MCMLXII — Trans-Lux Television Corporation
All Rights Reserved — Under License, CLEINMAN & SONS, PROVIDENCE, R. I.

NO. 3109

The animated adventures of the Mighty Hercules spawned this show accurate Magic Ring, which gave children the delusion of super strength Herc, super strength Herc. Canadians will get that reference.

Everybody Shout!
These fun PVC figures based on the 1971
Filmation series "The Groovie Goolies"
were made by Chem Toy.

Clockwise from Top Left:
Mummy, Drac, Hagatha, Wolfie and Bella La Ghostly.

These 1972 Larami Musical Horns had little-to-no connection to Hanna-Barbera's The Banana Splits once removed from the package.

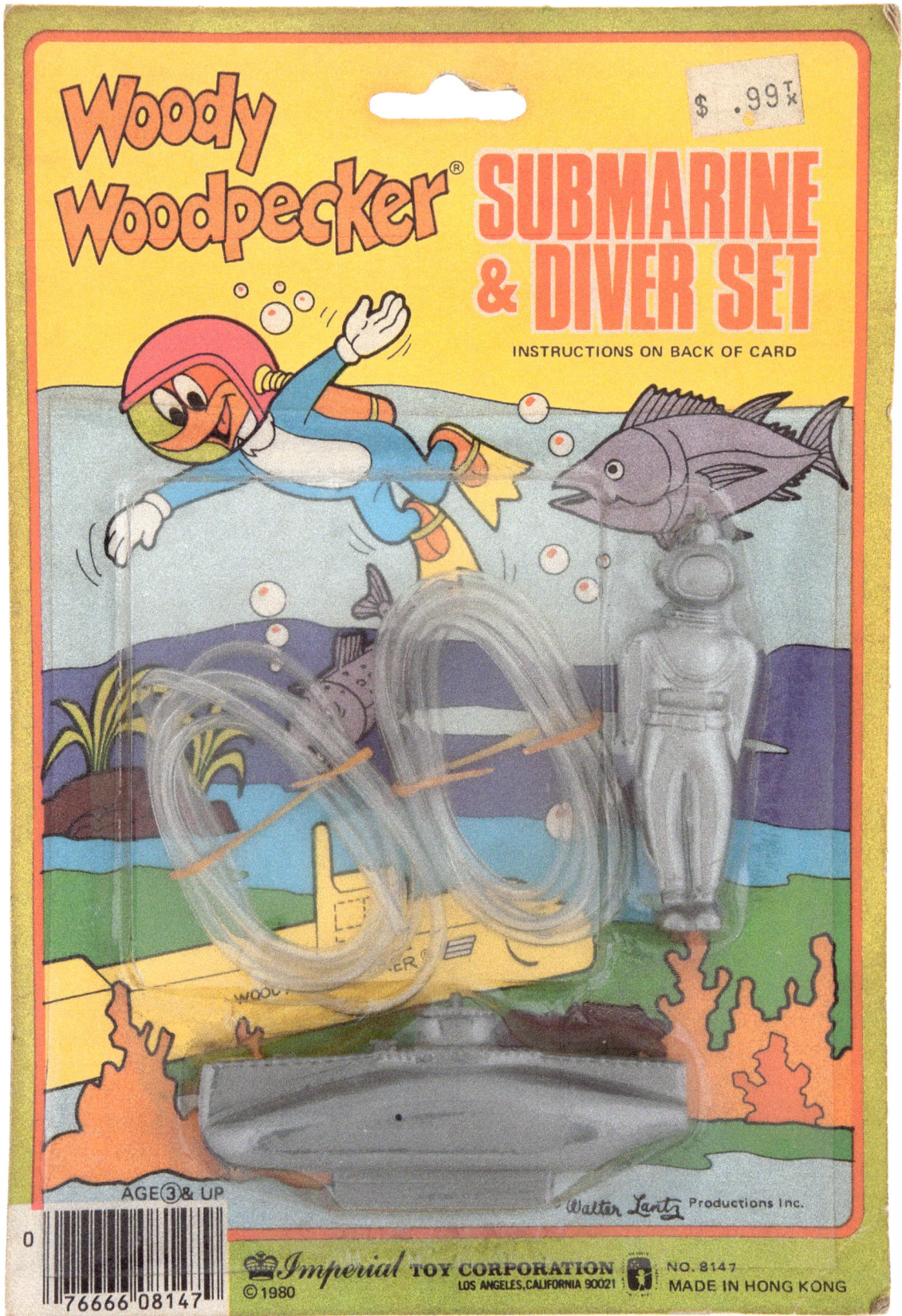

When kids hear Woody Woodpeckers' name, they should immediately think "Deep Sea Diving" or at least that's what Imperial Toys hoped when they released this weird set in 1980.

This 1971 set from Larami combined the then popularity of Penelope Pitstop with the Hippie

JOSIE AND THE PUSSY CATS

© MCMLXXII HANNA-BARBERA PRODS., INC.
RADIO COMICS, INC.

PENDANT JEWELRY SET

CAUTION: NOT RECOMMENDED FOR CHILDREN UNDER 3 YEARS OF AGE

WITH NEW ALL-IN-ONE SAFE MIRROR-COMB

ITEM NO. 9033 · LARAMI CORP. PHILA. PA. 19107   MADE IN HONG KONG

Left:

Josie and the Pussy Cats' appeal to girls was put to good use by Larami in 1974 with a series of items like this funky Pendant Jewelry set.

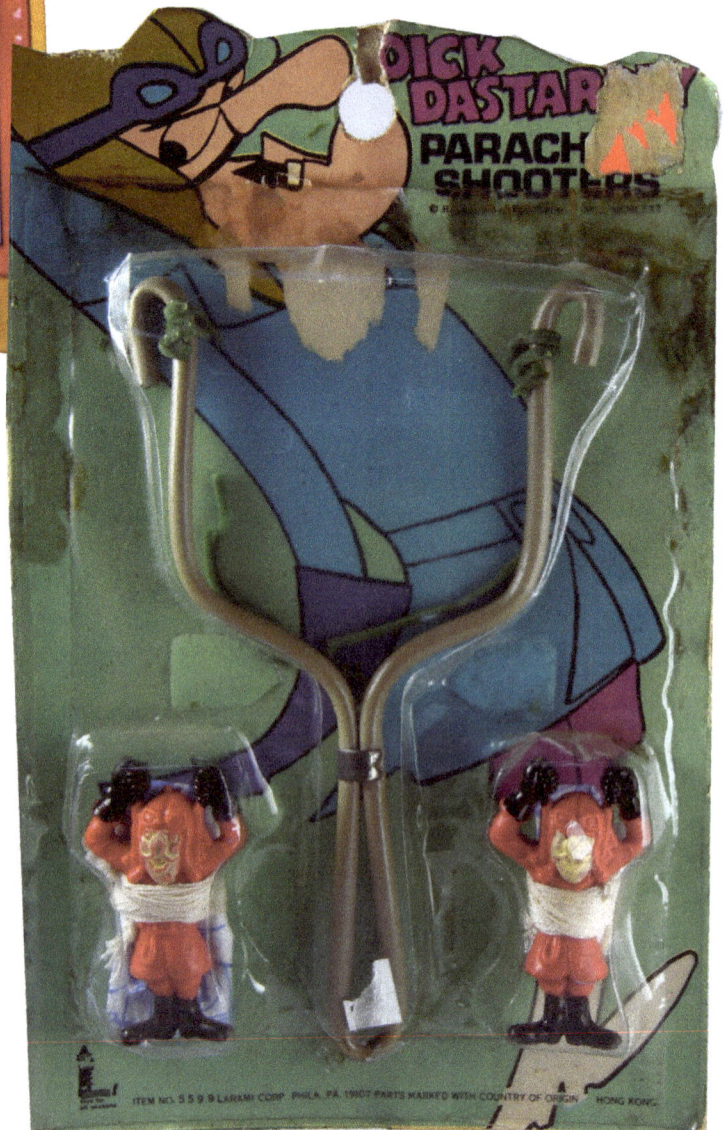

DICK DASTARDLY PARACHUTE SHOOTERS

ITEM NO. 5599 LARAMI CORP. PHILA. PA. 19107 PARTS MARKED WITH COUNTRY OF ORIGIN   HONG KONG

Right:

Cartoon Super Villain Dick Dastardly was popular enough to get his own fun items like these 1971 Parachute Shooters by Larami Toys.

An assortment of Hanna-Barbera World Champion Sky Divers from the 1978 Imperial Toys Catalog. I guess Fred jumped off a Pterodactyl or something.

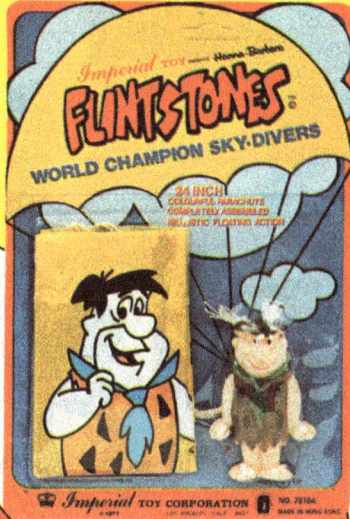

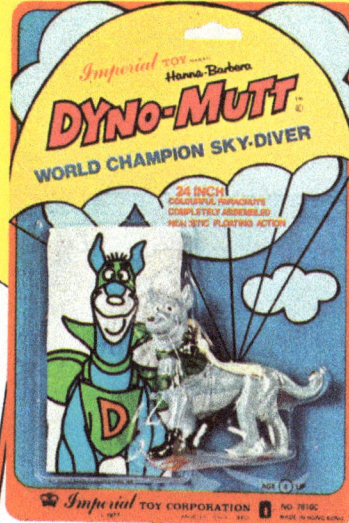

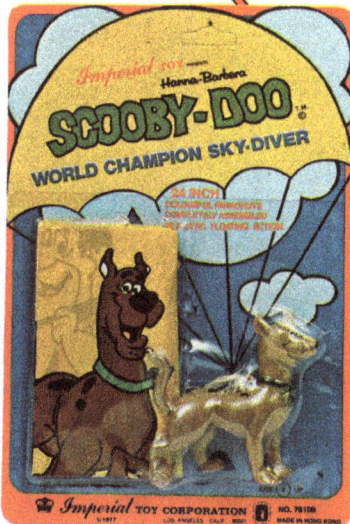

No. 8060-6
SIGNAL GUN
PK: 2 doz.
Card Size B 6" x 10"

No. 9526-5 $1.00
MOON SPINNERS
PK: 1 doz./12 doz.
Card Size B 6" x 10"

No. 8067-1 $1.29
JUNGLE EXPLORER
PK: 1 doz./12 doz.
Card Size C 7¼" x 10½"

LAND OF THE LOST ©

SAFARI SHOOTER

No. 8034-1 $1.29
PREHISTORIC
MONSTERS
PK: 1 doz./12 doz.
Card Size B 5" x 10"

No. 9514-1 $1.00
WILDERNESS CAMPER
PK: 2 doz./12 doz.
Card Size C 6" x 10½"

No. 7046-6 79¢
FLYING SAUCER GUN
PK: 2 doz./24 doz.
Card Size B 6" x 10"

A 1976 assortment of Larami Toys based on the Saturday morning series Land of the Lost. It was rumored that a dispute over royalties on these very toys caused series lead actor Spencer Milligan to depart the series.

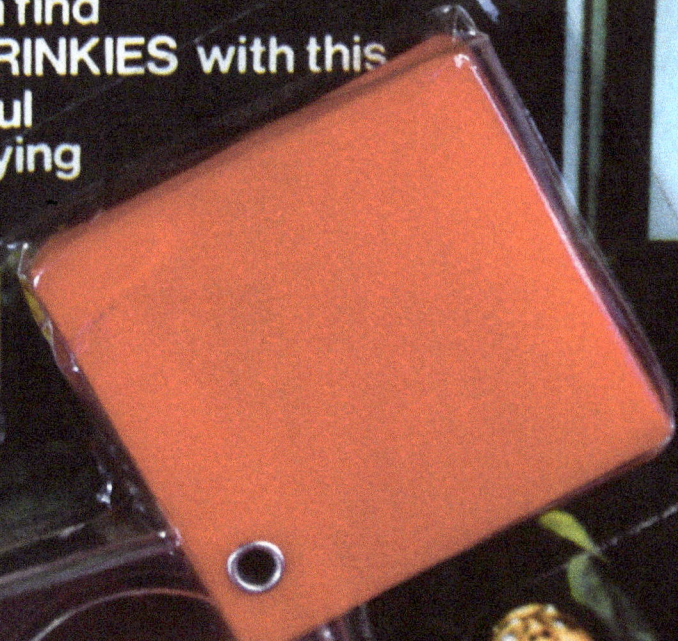

Dr. Shrinker was a 15 minute segment of the "Krofft Supershow" and this clever 1977 Magnifying Glass by Harmony is one of the only items licensed for this show.

119

A surprisingly show accurate toy from Harmany.

ボーリング
ポンプ

スペクトルマン

正義の使者

BOWLING PUMP ©フジテレビ

Above:
*A Water Gun Bowling
Pump of Japanese
hero Supekutoruman
(Spectreman in North
America) produced in
1971. The manfacturer
is unknown.*

Left:
*A Japanese figural
watergun of popular
space cop Urutoraman
(Ultra-Man),
manufacturer and date
unknown.*

Left:

A display of Larami Popeye merchandise, most of them bubble related, from the 1986 catalog.

Above:

A Bubble Pipe from the 1960s cashing in on the sailor man's filthy habit.

Above:

This 1980 set from Larami Toys gives you the ability to shave Popeye's enormous chin.

Above:

Imperial Toy Super 7 Boys Watch of Superhero Manta from the Manta & Moray segment. This is one of the only licensed products known to exist from the Saturday morning program.

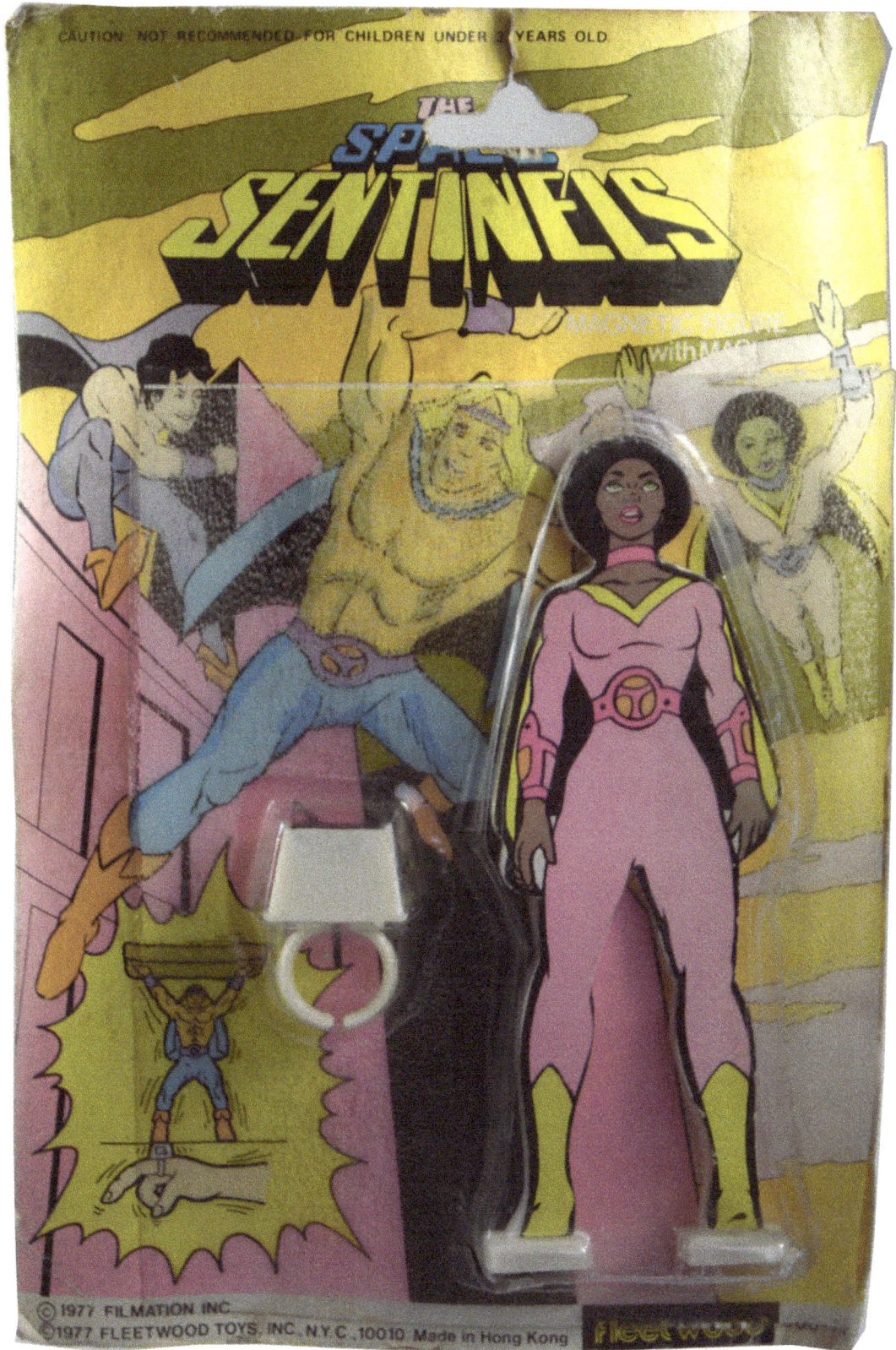

Above:

The syndicated Filmation series Space Sentinels was popular enough to see some fun products from Fleetwood in 1977. This figure is of Astrea, one third of the trio.

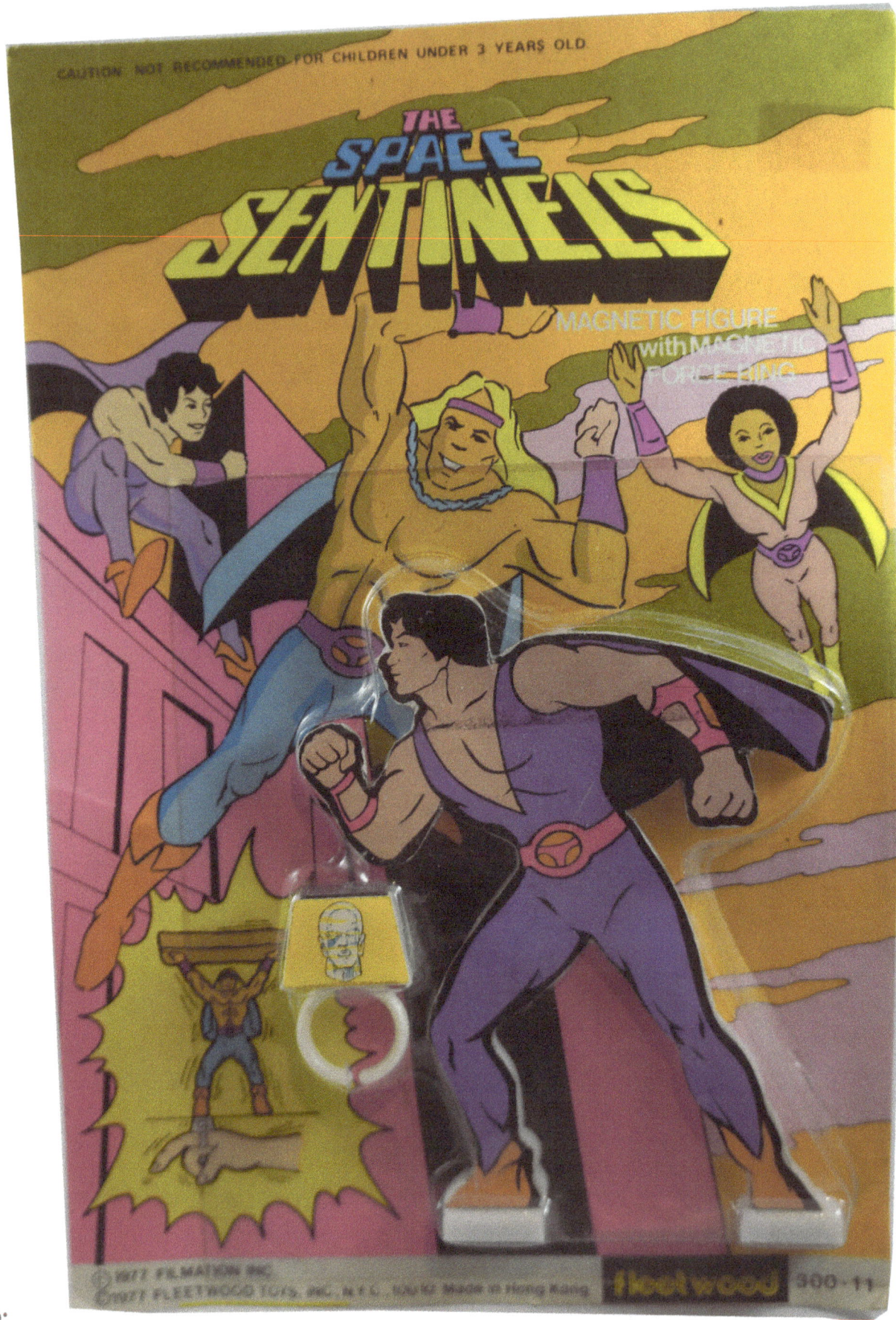

Above:
Mercury (this page) and Hercules (overleaf) round out the team.

The puppet adventures of Captain Scarlet spawned several fun, lower cost vehicles by Lincoln International in 1967.

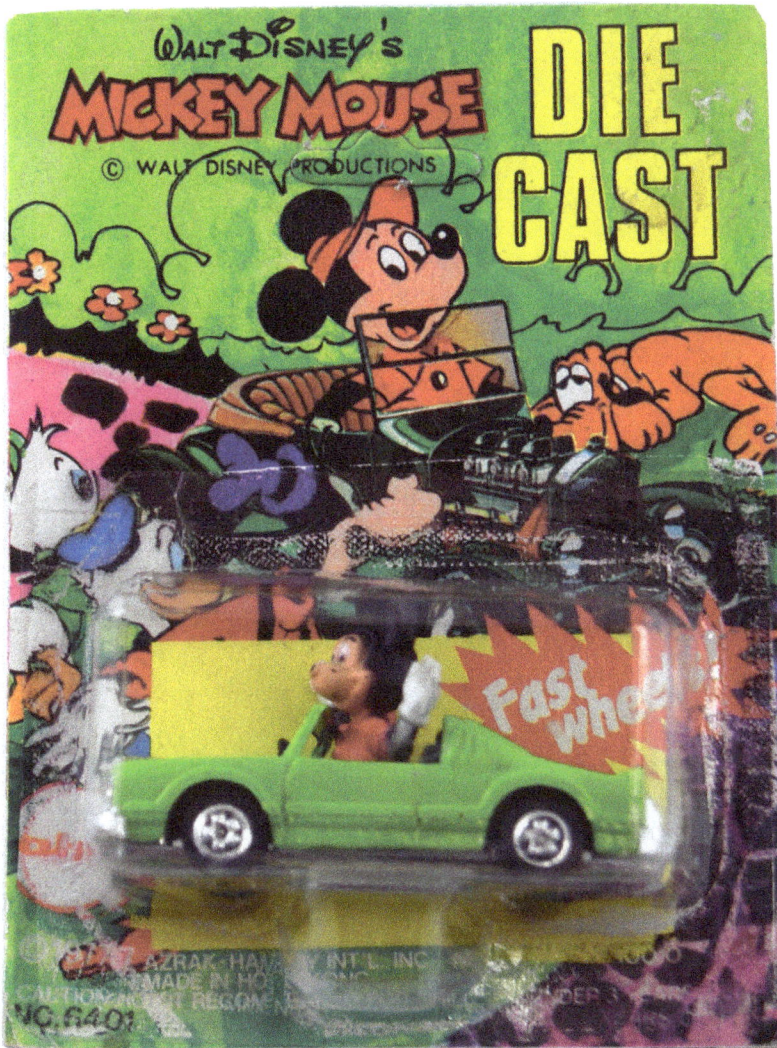

The Magic Kingdom

Even the populace of the magic kingdom are no strangers to lower cost goods. Disney characters have been Rack Toy staples for decades.

Above:
A Mickey Mouse die cast Fast Wheels car by AHI in 1974. The company would utilize the Disney license for the majority of the decade.

Right:
Donald Duck Flashlight Fun Face, produced by Arco in the 1980s.

Chapter Six
Generic Joy

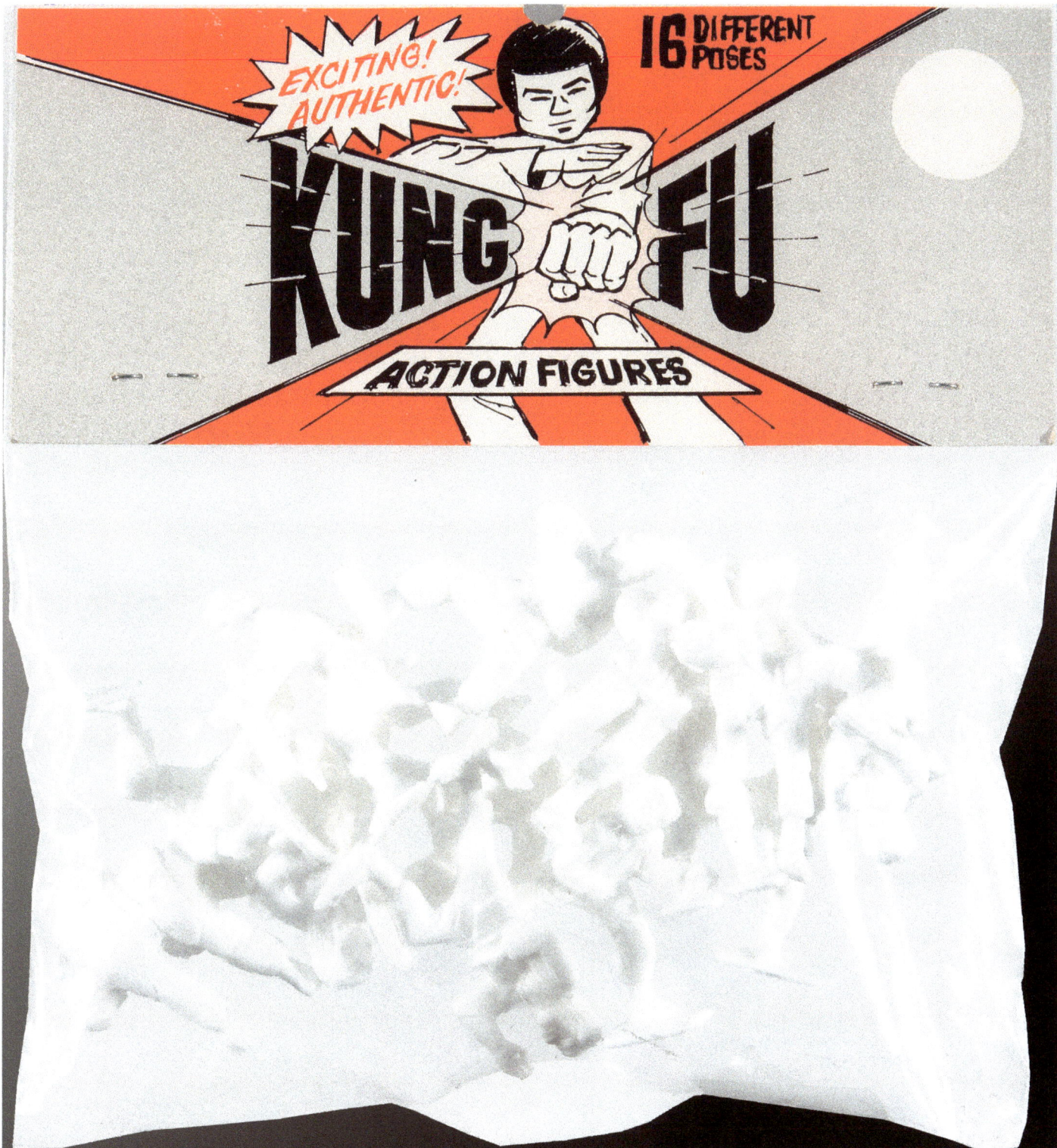

Sometimes the simple pleasures are the best ones...

Rack Toys need not be about licenses; many times the basic charm of green plastic army men, squirt guns or rubber bugs is enough.

Readily available for decades, the products will likely remain so for the foreseeable future. Many companies such as Imperial Toy Corporation have made their business on such "evergreen" items.

Sutton Plastics Kung Fu Action Figures combined the mid 70s martial arts craze to an old favorite, the plastic army man.

Pooper Power

Imperial Toys sold the Poopatrooper brand in different incarnations for over 30 years, beginning in 1971.

The Troopers were sold in numerous ways, with this counter display being the most common.

THE DEATH OF A FLY
"SPOORY SPIDER"

MADE IN HONG KONG

THE Hungry Mouse in the Cheese House

49¢

Imperial TOY CORPORATION
No. 404   LOS ANGELES, CALIF. 90021

Above:
Rubber mice with rubber cheese by Imperial Toy in 1970.

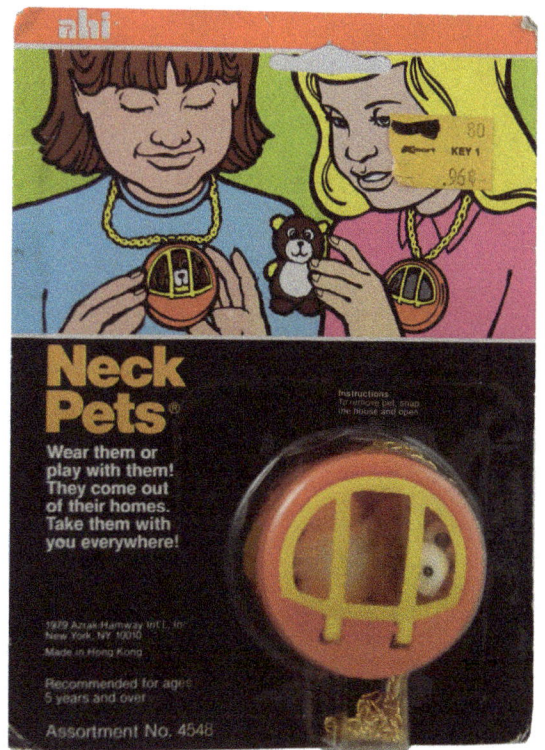

ahi

Neck Pets®
Wear them or play with them! They come out of their homes. Take them with you everywhere!

1979 Azrak-Hamway Int'l, Inc.
New York, NY 10010

Made in Hong Kong

Recommended for ages 5 years and over

Assortment No. 4548

Above:
One of the thousands of ways a rubber spider has been marketed. Manufacturer and date unknown.

Right:
Neck Pets by AHI in 1979 was an attempt to not scare little girls with tiny creatures.

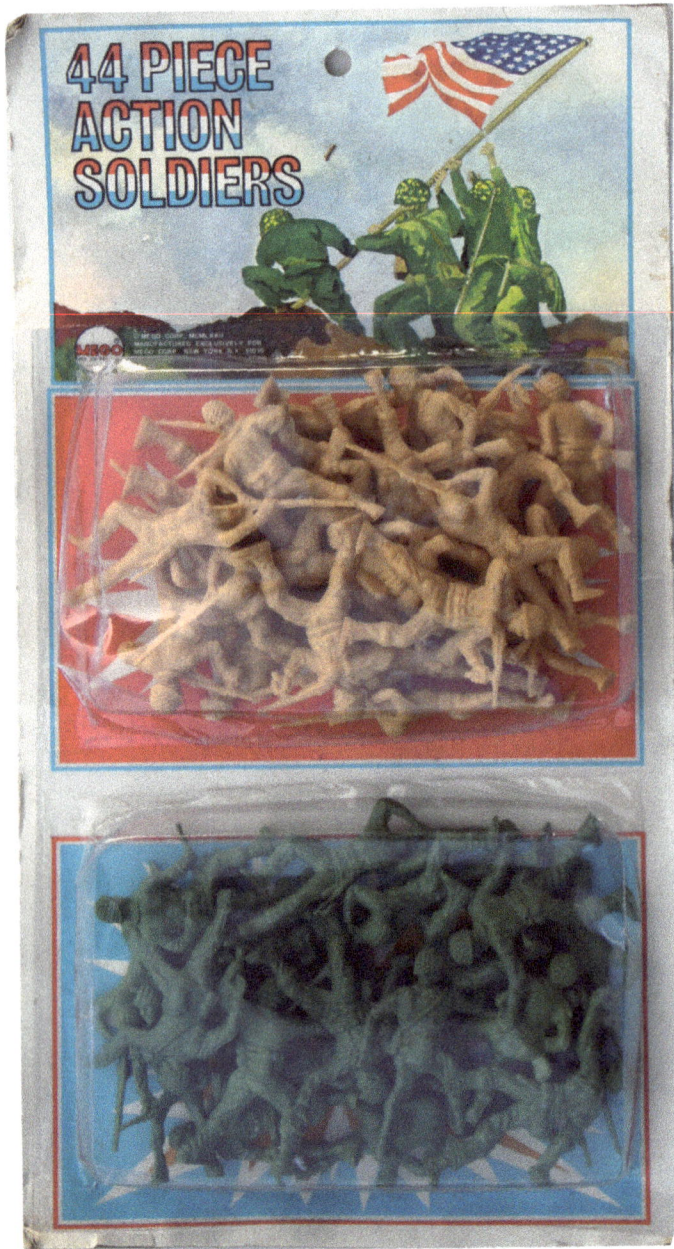

44 PIECE ACTION SOLDIERS

Soldiers in Action

RIFLE FIRING Soldier

Model weapon really shoots bullets!

CAUTION: NOT RECOMMENDED FOR CHILDREN UNDER 3 YEARS

CAT. NO. 2100 © 1975 ... NAL LTD. MADE IN HONG KONG

LINCOLN INTERNATIONAL

★ **MILITARY HEADQUARTERS** ★

The green plastic army man has been a dime store staple since the 1950s. Produced in hundreds of forms by dozens of manufacturers, they could fill an entire book of their own.

Above:
44 pieces of Military Action produced by the Mego Corporation in 1970.

Above Right:
1975 Rifle Firing Soldier by Lincoln International.

Right:
A Ja-Ru military display from 1986, a time where military toys were once again in vogue.

Above:

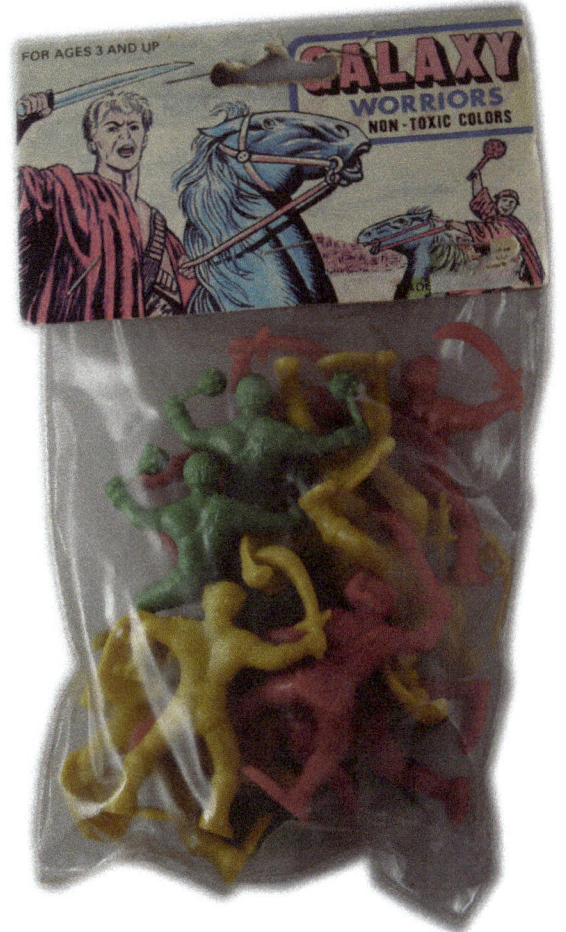

The space race was popular on the playground, as evidenced by these Space Heroes figures produced by Payton in the 1960s.

Above Right:

Some of the earliest toys produced by Imperial cashed in on the Moon Landing.

Right:

The Galaxy "Worriors" are recycled fantasy characters hastily slapped together to capitilize on the popularity of Star Wars.

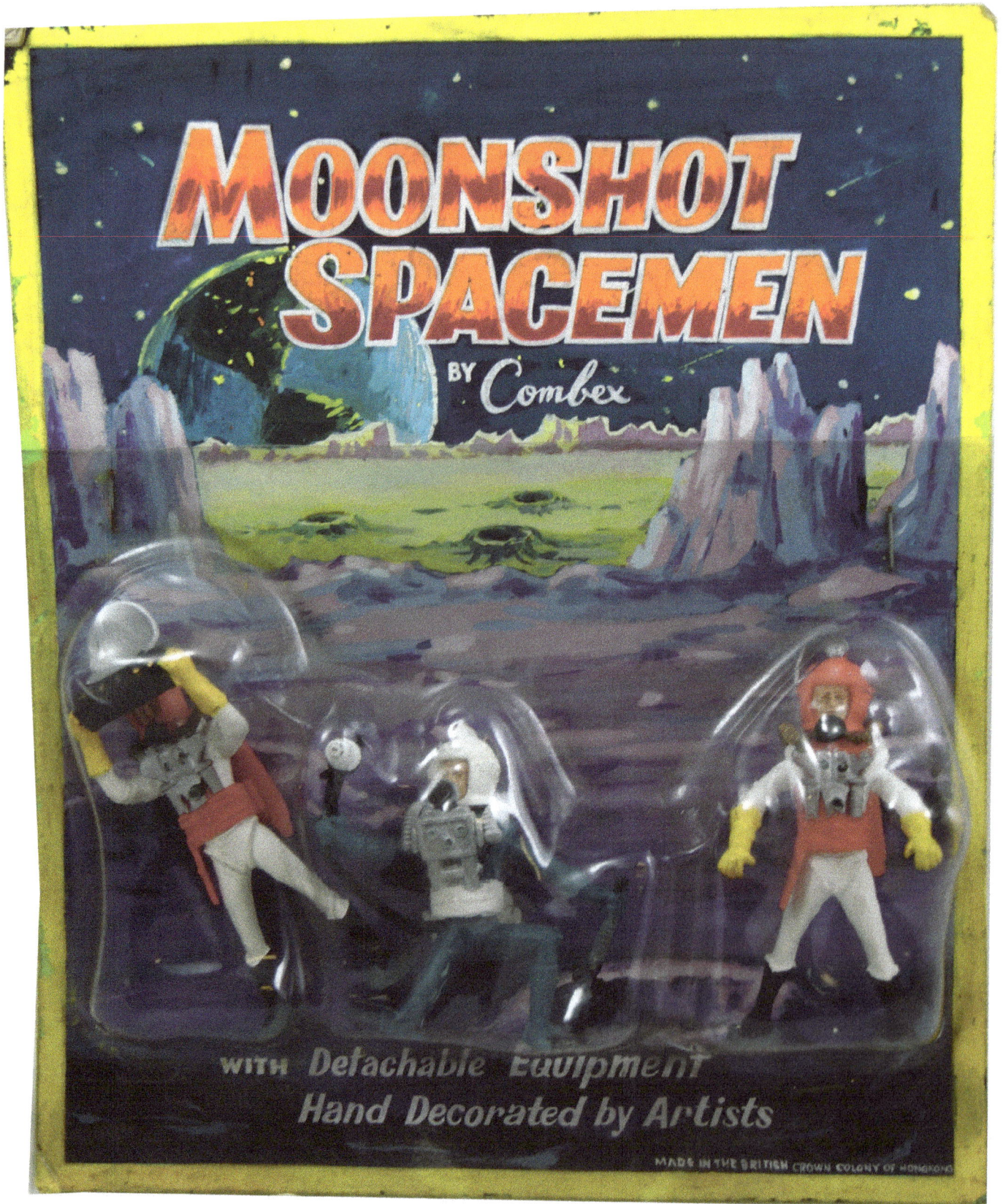

These Moonshot Spacemen from Combex date back to the 1960s. This isn't a factory made item, but rather a sales sample. The cardback is actually hand painted and you can see the brush strokes on the cardstock.

PROJÈTE DES MISSILES !
PLIS LES AILES !

SHOOTING MISSILES !
FOLDING WINGS !

SPACE

DIE CAST METAL ★ FREE RUNNING WHEELS
EN MÉTAL MOULÉ ★ ROUES LIBRES

MASTER

2002 M.O.

CAUTION: NOT RECOMMENDED FOR
CHILDREN UNDER 3 YEARS OLD

MADE IN HONG KONG
FABRIQUÉ À HONG KONG

NOBILITY®

P. O. BOX 330
POINTE CLAIRE, QUE.

Space Master 2002 was one of many late 70s toys hoping to cash in on the science fiction craze of the late 1970s.

135

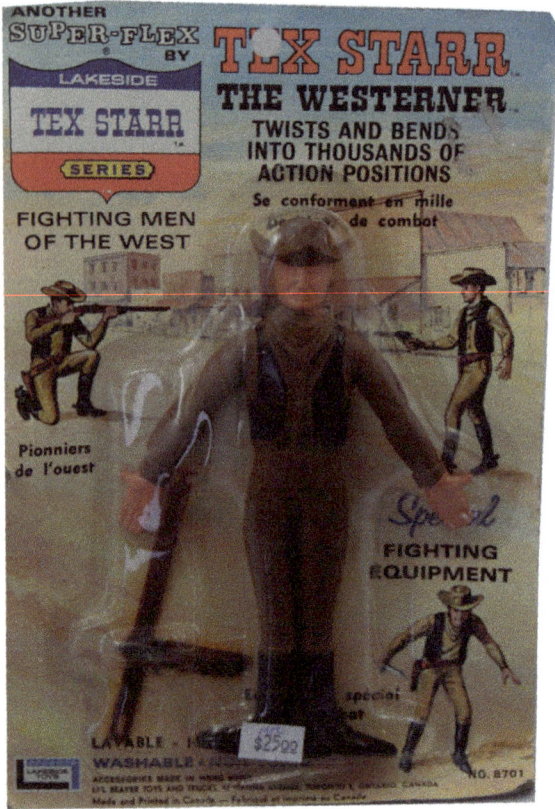

Above and Below:
The Tex Starr Super-Flex line by Lakeside was probably only sold in Canada during the late 1960s.

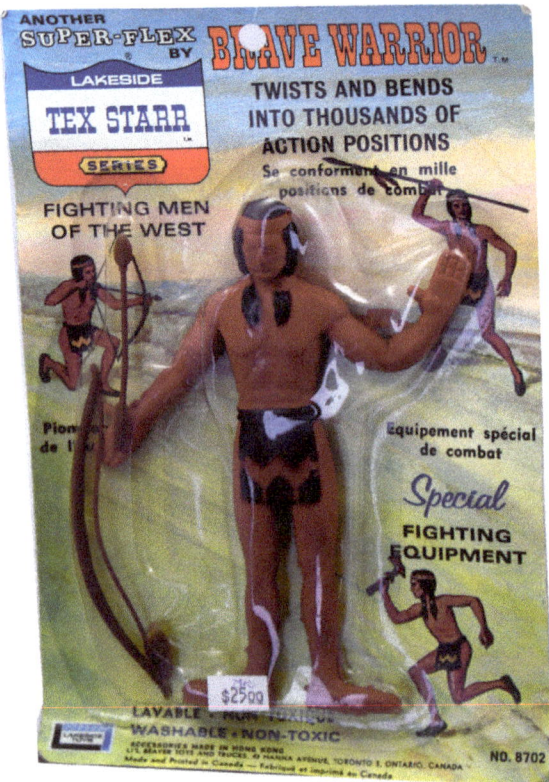

Above:
This Chief Crazy Horse figure is believed to be from the early 1960s; the manfacturer is unknown..

Right:

A standard Squirt Gun by Zee Toys. The s card art makes it pretty obvious that it was made in the 1970s.

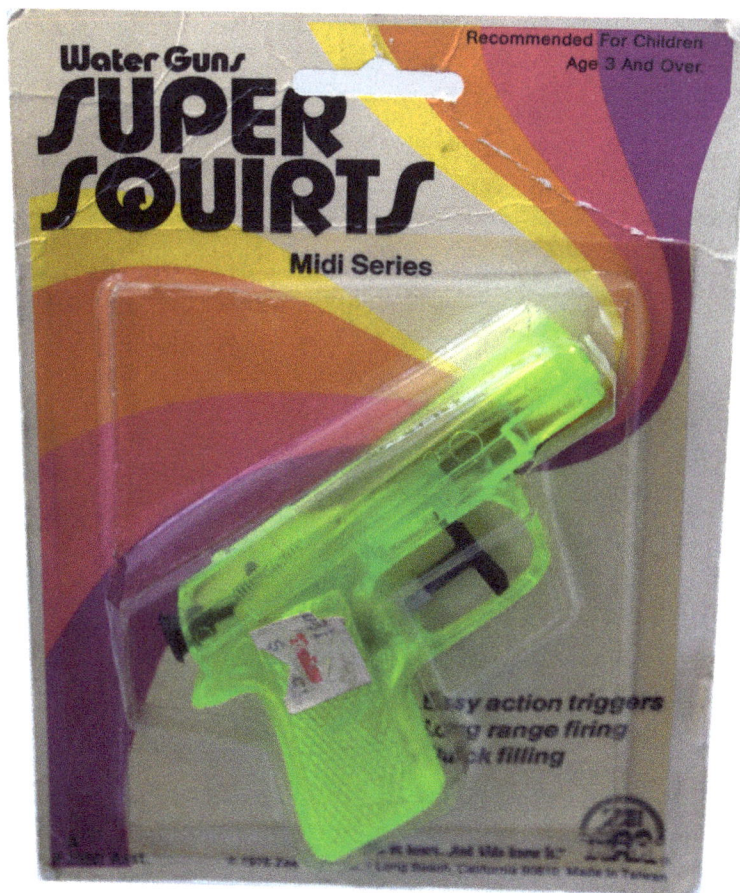

Above:

Jak-Pak's Squirt Rings made for hilarious engagement pranks in 1977.

Right:

A selection of generic Water Guns with eye popping card artwork from the 1976 Larami Toy Catalog.

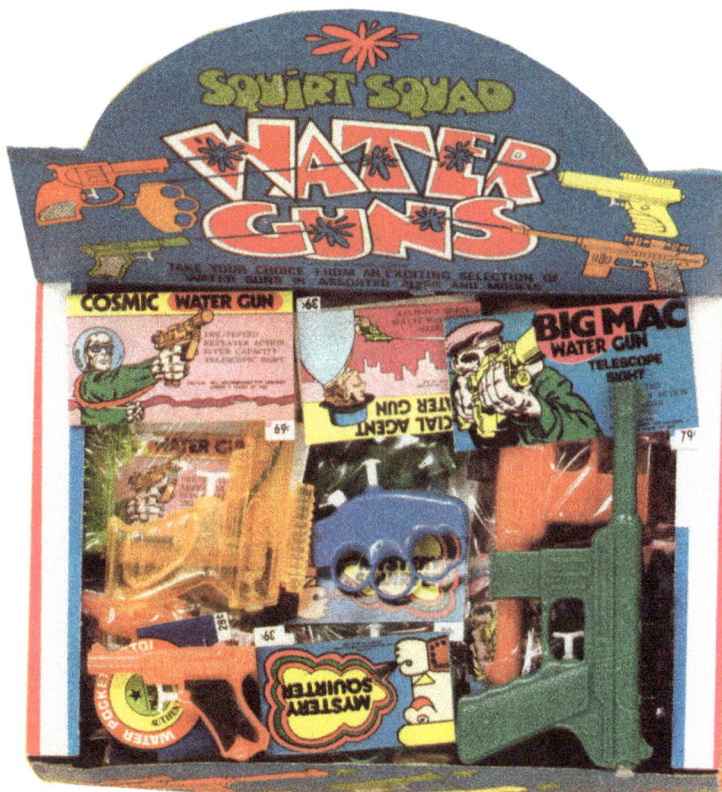

SANTA PUTTY ™

The EGG-SHAPED Santa with Putty inside!

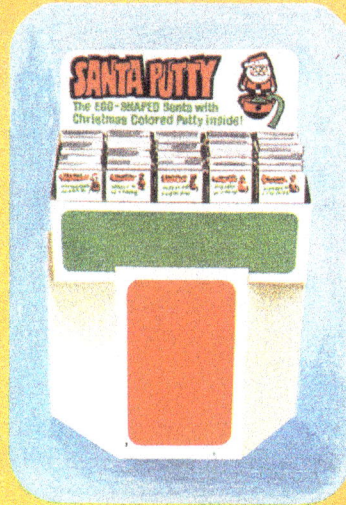

#8930 SANTA PUTTY FLOOR DISPLAY

Packed in a self contained, easily set up floor display containing 8 dz. packages. Packed 3 displays (individually reshippable) per master carton, weight 45 lbs.

#8931 SANTA PUTTY COUNTER DISPLAY

Packed 2 dz. per full-color self-containted counter display. 6 deals per master carton (12 dz.).

#893 SANTA PUTTY

Blister packed on a double sided 5 x 7 card. Packed 2 dz. per re-shippable inner carton. 24 dz. per master carton, weight 42 lbs.

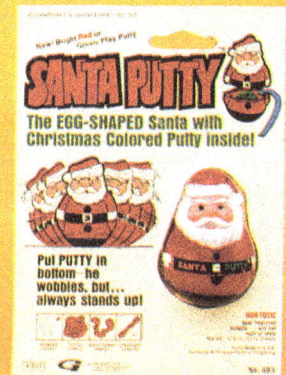

STRETCHES · BOUNCES · COPIES · SHAPES

Henry Gordy's Santa Putty is probably not as gross as it sounds...

Chapter Seven
Hey, Knock it Off!

Bootleg, Howl.

There will always be imitators and in the world of toys, copying or mimicking someone else's idea is still a daily occurrence.

Rack Toys are especially plagued with cheap simulations of the real thing. Manufacturers names are often left off the packaging in a wonderful "fly by night" fashion.

The mix of boldness and cheapness often results in hilarity, with products that are uniquely collectible in their own right.

Above:
Joe, Pat, Gus and Bingo were a lesser known quartert from Liverpool; manufacturer and date unknown.

Right:
Ben Cooper didn't have the Jaws license in 1975 but upped the play value by adding a delicious swimmer.

The wild popularity of Batman over the decades has seen an abundance of knock offs, many of them quite blatant adding to the absurdity..

Above:

This ludicrous BatMan water pistol from the 1960s has deservedly garnered a lot of attention for the placement of the trigger and water hole.

Left:

Two 1960s Batman knockoffs that substitute "Bat" with "Space". Don't try and think about why-you'll just get a nosebleed.

Left:

This Green Arrow Archery Set bears no copyright or manufacturer name. Green Arrow fans, however, welcomed its discovery as the character didn't see much legitimate merchandise.

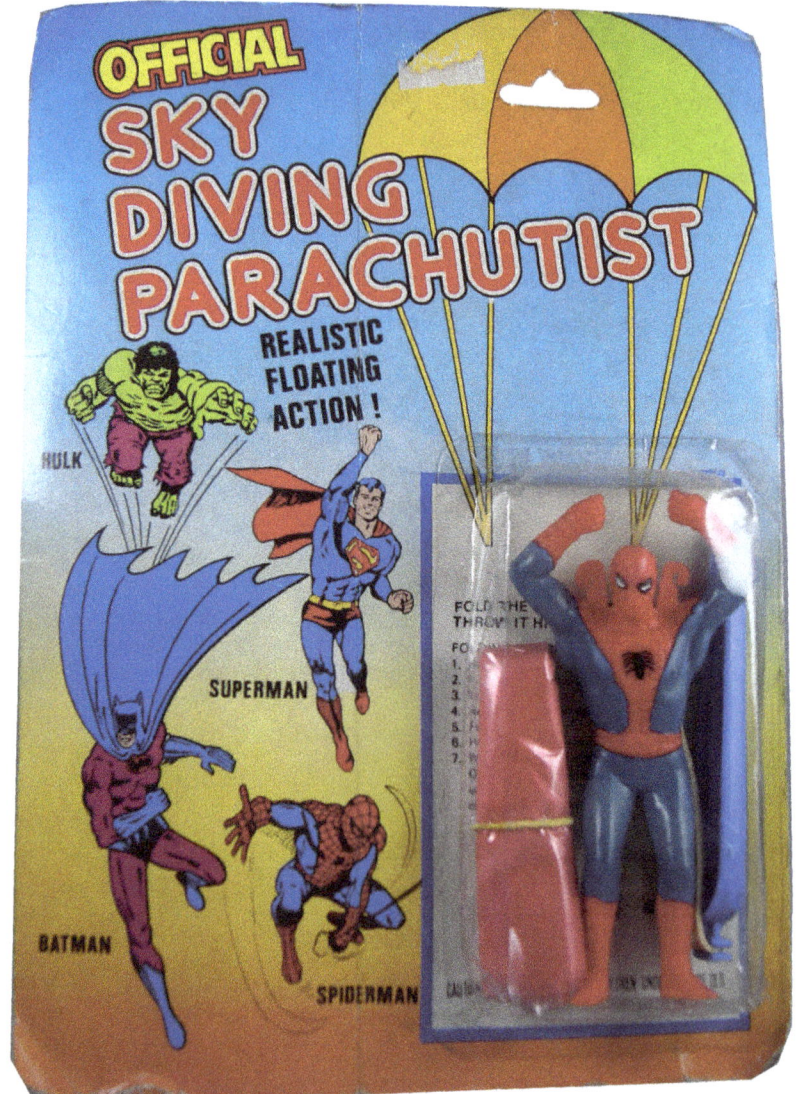

Above:

This Spider-Man Parachutist from the 1980s was made from the AHI molds, but the lack of copyright information combined with it's misspelling of "SpiderMan" reveal it as a rather bold bootleg item.

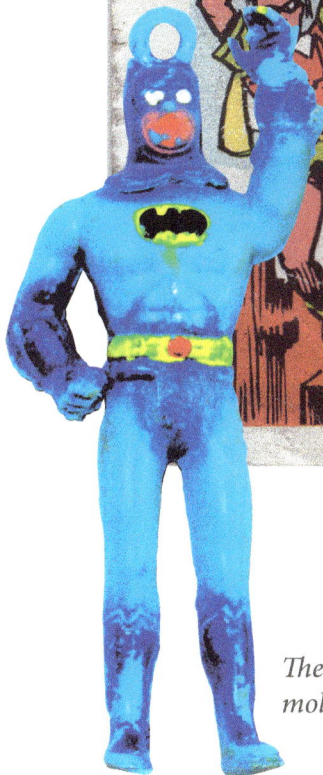

These Mexican Parachute figures from 1980 were actually blow molded copies of Mego Pocket Superheroes Action Figures.

Above:
This Super Flyer advises you to enjoy it on a spacious plain. Judging how annoyed Superman looks, you better do what he says kids.

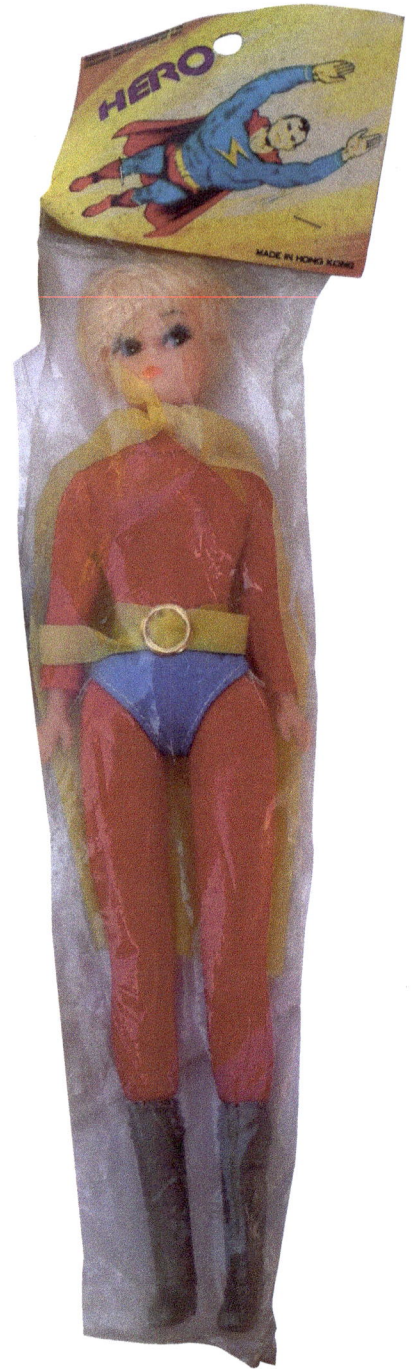

Above:
This blow molded Hero figure is nothing more than a Fashion Doll with a Superhero slant. .

Left:
This Space Visitor figure comes from Italy and is believed to be from the late 1970s. The head is a direct copy of a Mego Superman action figure.

This dynamic duo are hollow blow molded figures wearing what appears to be left over clothes from Ideal's Captain Action and Mego's World's Greatest Superheroes. Cheap figures wearing factory seconds were a prevalent phenomenon during the 1970s.

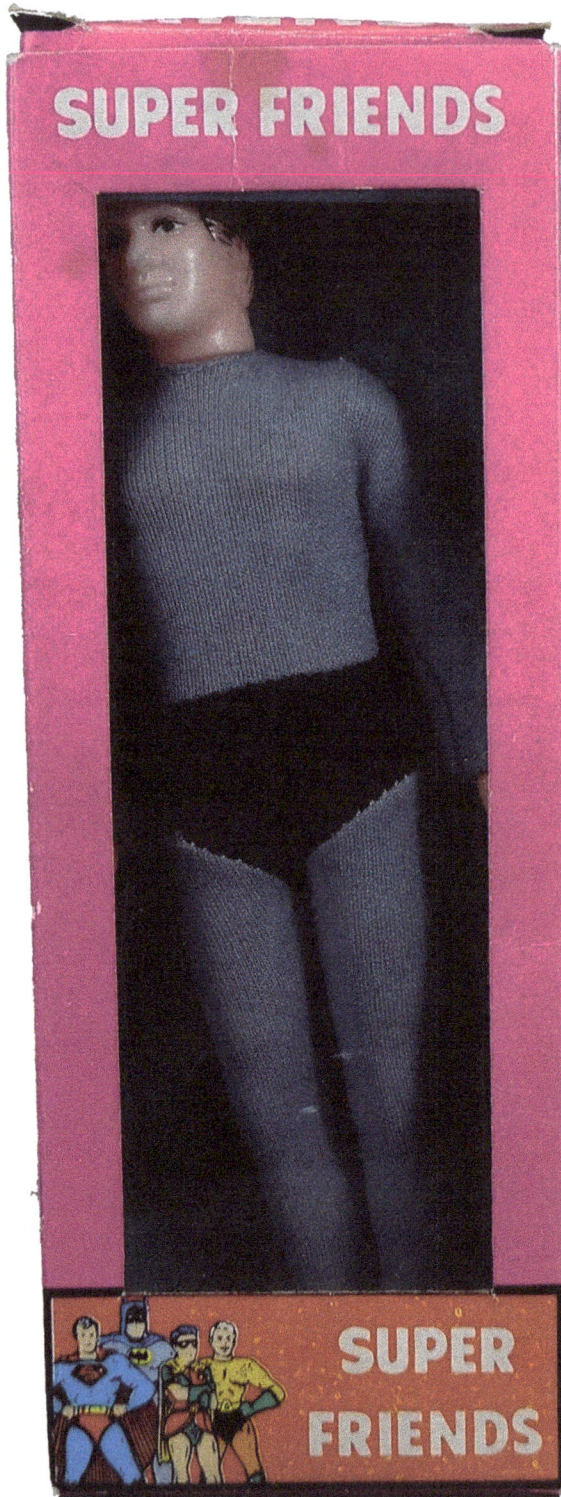

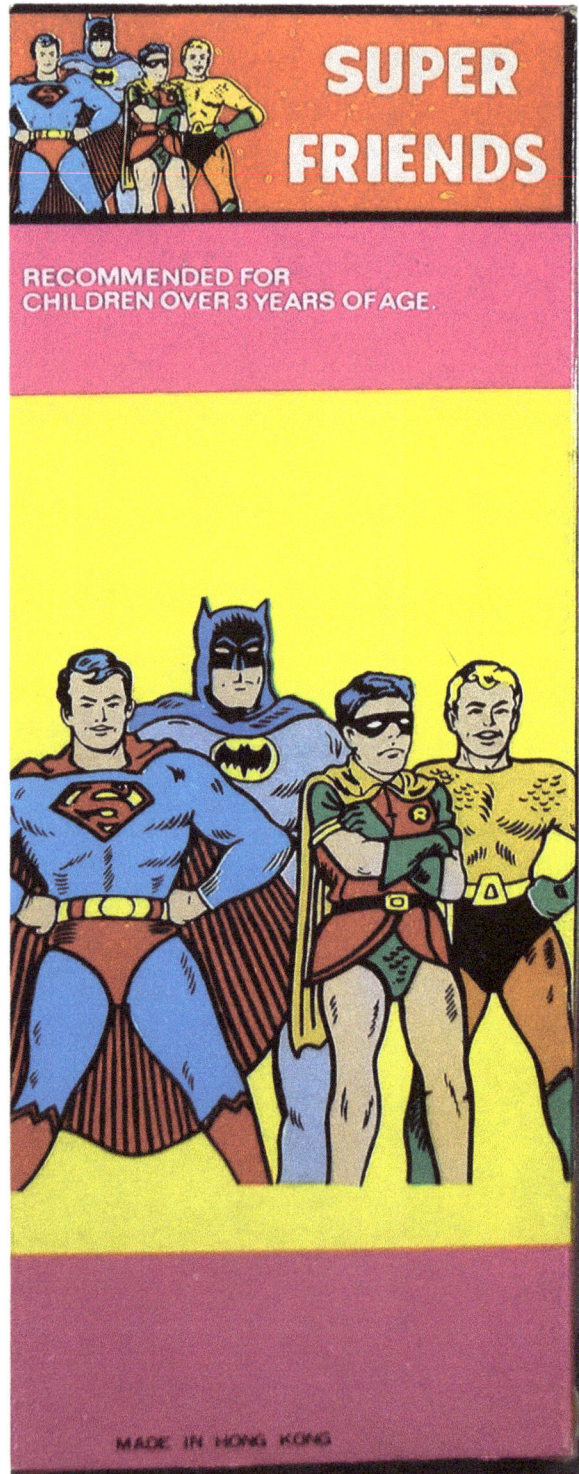

Super Friends are cheap plastic dolls wearing left over costumes from Mego superheroes.
They are wonderful and I love them

Everybody went Ape
The 1970s Planet of the Apes craze caused several toy manufacturers to create Apes of their own. This included AHI, whose "Action Apemen" briefly mingled with the officially licensed Planet of the Apes products they manufactured.

Above:
Astro Apes' Artemus action figure produced by United Manufacturing Company in 1974, although they left their name off the packaging.

AHI "Action Apeman" figures were stopped by a legal injunction from Mego and 20th Century Fox.

The Electrogenic Arm was Florida based toy maker FunStuf's way of exploiting the popularity of the "Six Million Dollar Man" series without paying licensing fees.

Sonic Man and Sonic Woman produced by Tomland, are obviously brazen attempts to cash in on the popularity of The Six Million Dollar Man and The Bionic Woman.

Caution : Not recommended for children under 3 years of age.

SONIC
WOMAN

Fully jointed
woman of the future

© Tomland 1977

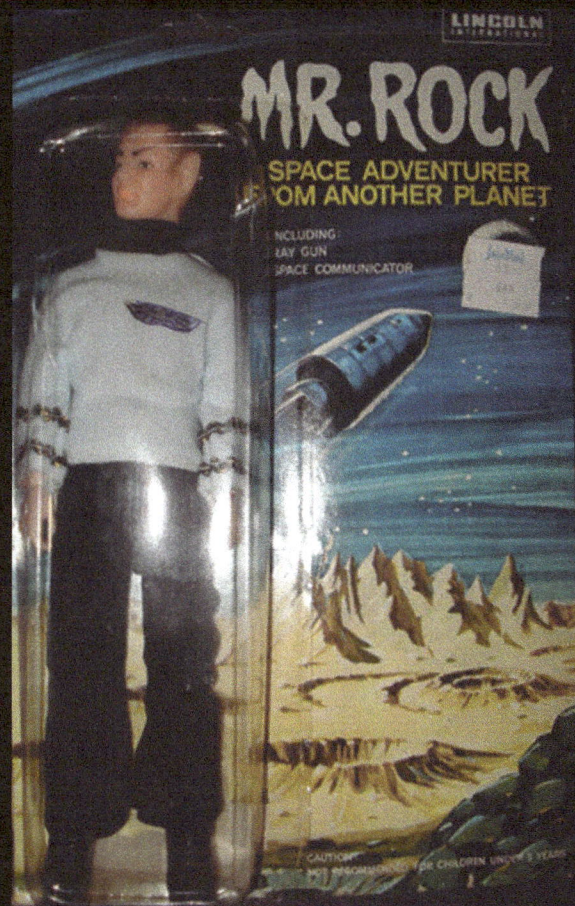

MR. ROCK

SPACE ADVENTURER FROM ANOTHER PLANET

INCLUDING:
RAY GUN
SPACE COMMUNICATOR

Mr. Rock was a blatant copy of Star Trek's most popular character, produced by Lincoln International in 1976.

Ironically, the unlicensed Mr Rock figure commands a much higher value on the collector's market than the officially licensed version of Mr Spock produced by Mego Toys.

CAUTION: NOT RECOMMENDED FOR CHILDREN UNDER 3 YEARS OLD

GALAXY LASER TEAM
with space monsters

26 PCS.

Tim Mee TOYS

TIM MEE TOYS
MONTGOMERY, ILLINOIS 60538

NO. 0931

Above:

Galaxy Laser Team by Tim Mee Toys had some Wookie like characters, many such toys created in the late 1970s as a reaction to the popularity of Star Wars.

Right:

Tomland Toys Starroid Raider action figure, a line that seemed to exist mainly to confuse well meaning grandparents.

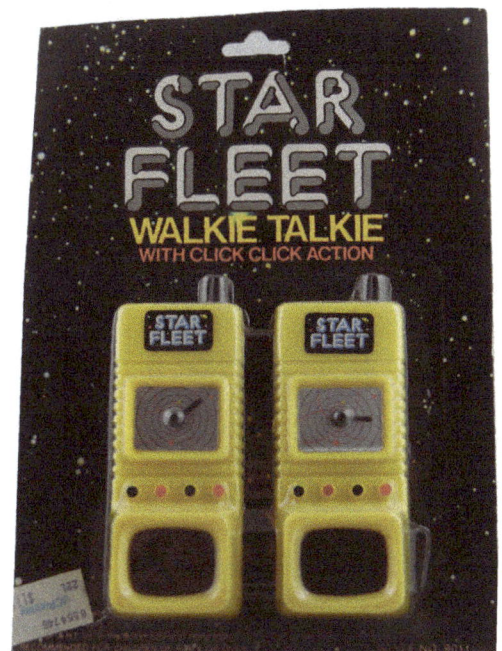

Above:
Larami Toys marketed Star Fleet items in 1979, which implied some sort of connection to Star Trek. The logo cleverly aped the title design from Space:1999. Two shows with one toy-nice!!

Above:
AHI also had their own line of Star Fleet toys and action figures in 1979. Great minds think alike.

Right:

These Mexican produced figures have bodies from the Battlestar Galactica Cylon and heads from the Planet of the Apes. It's the crossover series we can only dream of...

Right:

These Mexican produced figures have bodies from the Battlestar Galactica Cylon and heads from the Planet of the Apes. It's the crossover series we can only dream of...

154

Wrestling Super Stars

CHIEF IRONHEAD

Twist and Turn them into All Kinds Of Wrestling Holds

VIKTOR VULGAR

Twist and Turn them into All Kinds Of Wrestling Holds

BRUTE BRUCE

Twist and Turn them into All Kinds Of Wrestling Holds

BEARDED BOMBER

Twist and Turn them into All Kinds Of Wrestling Holds

SCARY HAIRY

Twist and Turn them into All Kinds Of Wrestling Holds

MASKED MARVIN

Twist and Turn them into All Kinds Of Wrestling Holds

SUPER STARS
6 Asst.
#33010
Card Size 6 x 7

FIRST AID KIT

FIRST AID KIT

FIRST AID KIT
#33020
Card Size 6 x 10

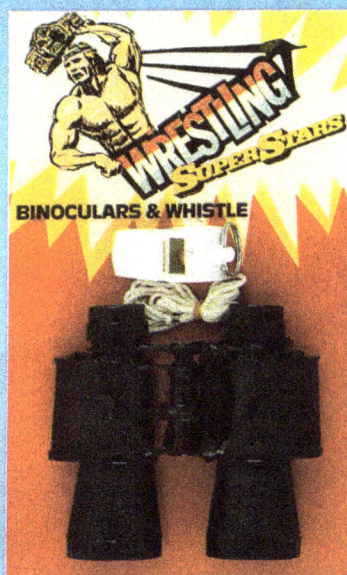

BINOCULARS & WHISTLE

BINOCULARS & WHISTLE
#33030
Card Size 6 x 10

TIMEKEEPER SET

TIMEKEEPER SET
#33040
Card Size 6 x 10

Page 3

A rather bold swipe on the WWE by Larami.

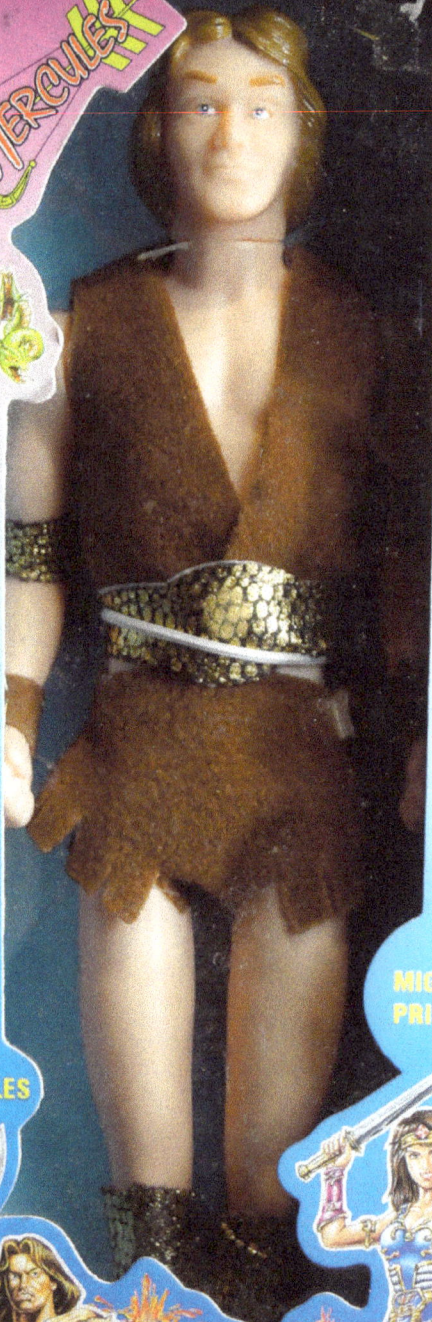

CLASSIC CHARACTER SERIES

HERCULES

HERCULES

MIGHTY PRINCESS

Hercules and his companion Mighty Princess started popping up in dollar stores in the late 1990s, their resemblance to then-popular television shows I'm sure is purely coincidental

⚠ WARNING: CHOKING HAZARD—small parts. Not for Children under 3 yrs. For ages 4 and up

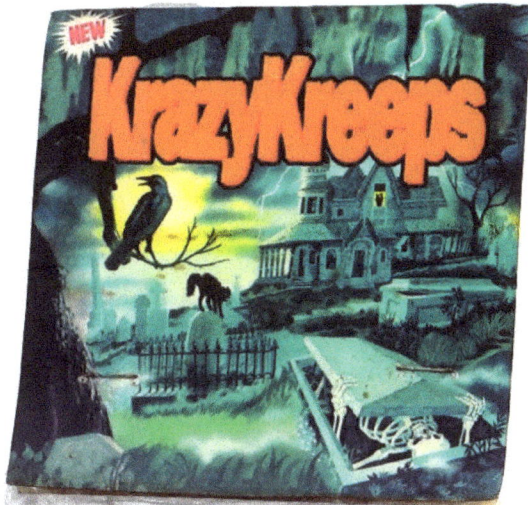

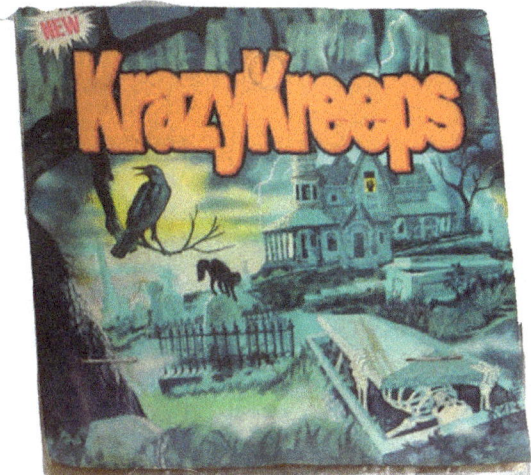

Krazy Kreeps are a curious item, made utilizing the molds of the AHI World Famous Super Monster Toys. Each figure has a tiny hang man's noose around its neck, a morbid little detail that surely wouldn't fly today.

Racking up Rack Toys

For me, toys bring us back to a time when we were younger, the world was a simpler place (at least it seemed that way), and the little pleasures somehow managed to give infinitely more satisfaction than most of the achievements you can attain as an adult. Which means that for me, the toys contained in this volume take me right back to Camp Becket.

Located (unsurprisingly) in the lovely little town of Becket, in western Massachusetts, Camp Becket was one of the highlights of my childhood. It's been there for more than a hundred years, and hopefully it'll be there for at least a hundred more. Camp Becket is the real deal. It's old school – there's no electricity, you live in the woods, zero creature comforts.

It's a life changing experience for anyone lucky enough to have been molded by their philosophies. A major hurdle for many who attend is a strict no soda rule. On top of all the other rules, that particular edict could seem like an effort to add insult to injury. But I absolutely loved the place. I can't say enough good things about Camp Becket, and I wouldn't trade all the summers I spent there for even one of Elon Musk's bank accounts. There might be a few toys I'd be willing to negotiate about, but that's a hypothetical I'll thankfully never have to actually grapple with.

A highlight of every summer at Camp Becket was the one occasion when we would leave camp and make our way into town. Becket was tiny, classic Americana, and my impression was that it couldn't have been home to more than eighty souls back then. (I looked it up just to see how reality compares to my recollections, and as of the 2010 census the population appeared to be hovering around 1,700 – subtract the intervening years and my estimate probably wasn't that far off). In any case, after weeks of living by candle and flashlight, doing battle with insects, and being exposed to the elements, hiking into town was a welcome reprieve.

This excursion represented a coveted, and only, taste of "soda" we would experience all summer, a small interlude during which we got the chance to reconnect with civilization. Chief among our collective deprivations was the aforementioned lack of soda, a condition everyone was eager to remedy with a visit to that revered Shangri-La of commerce; the Becket General Store.

In my memory, whenever you first set eyes on the store it radiated sunbeams accompanied by the sound of magisterial choral voices. You see, at Camp Becket we would all vie for a variety of little jobs that allowed us to earn some money. Small amounts, for sure, but we'd all save up what seemed like little fortunes with an eye toward the long-awaited day when we would make our way into town and cross the glorious threshold into Becket's unrivalled mercantile palace. We would cram into that store like a swarm of eager locusts. After fantasizing about candy bars and ice cream and slush puppies for weeks, the moment had finally arrived when we could all plunk down our hard-earned cash and reap delightful sugary rewards.

Except for me, it wasn't about soda, or another lemon lime slush puppy.

For me, the true wonders of the Becket General Store were contained in the wall of toys. Rack toys, to be precise! Modest-sized toys, to be sure. Small things some might dismissively refer to as knickknacks or tchotchkes. Every single one of my pennies went straight to the purchase of as many of those wonderful toys as I could afford.

The variety was amazing!

There were figures and cars and spaceships and even more things I couldn't have imagined before I laid eyes on them. They were based on everybody's favorite TV shows and movies, or looked like they were based on those same favorite TV shows and movies.

There were Star Trek phasers and Battlestar Galactica bubble blowers and Knight Rider flashlights. Perhaps best of all, there were James Bond "X-ray" sunglasses. There was a slew of other James Bond-inspired gadgets, like the action pen (invisible ink that really was invisible), a spy watch (whose hands didn't move), and a barely-accurate-ish replica of his Walther PPK!

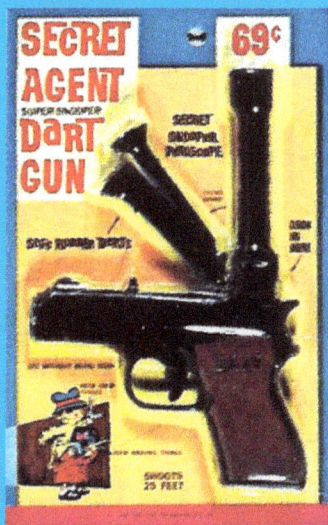

The acquisition of these items converted me into a crack double agent in one hour. Another summer I acquired dog tags and binoculars, preparing me to take on America's enemies, both foreign and domestic! There was also a short-lived obsession with a no-lens plastic telescope, too. As the years went by and I matured, I stopped buying these toys, but I never threw them out. I became what's now known as a "collector".

As I learned more and more about the industry and different brands, I kept hearing a term I was unfamiliar with – "rack toys". Imagine my delight when I figured out that this description referred specifically to the class of toys that I used to enthusiastically scoop up at my beloved Becket General Store! Learning that they occupied a special category of their own filled me with delight, somehow vindicating my cherished memories of those seemingly simple, disposable toys. All those gadgets based on my favorite television shows and movies were legitimately a thing of their own, and now I'm even writing an afterward to a book dedicated to documenting said toys in all their varied glory. Life can be a wonderful thing!

As my knowledge grew I did of course learn about that bastion of rack toy producers, the Larami Corp. In case you have already read this book but still aren't familiar with Larami, here's a quick rundown for you; eventually purchased by Hasbro in 1995 and finally wound down in 2002, Larami began way back in 1947.

Larami's stock in trade was low cost toys licensed from popular television shows and movies. (In later years they had huge success with another perennial favorite, the Super Soaker, but that's a topic for another Afterwards). You name it, they made a rack toy of it; Planet Of The Apes, Star Wars,

The A-Team, Batman, CHIPs, Land Of The Lost, Star Trek, Space:1999, and that's simple the tip of the rack-berg ¬– it's as if they were somehow able to channel my deepest toy desires directly from my head and materialize them into reality! And then those treasures would always find their way to the Becket General Store, where I could snap them up and round out my stellar summer camp experience.

One last thing about Larami – it's impossible to discuss the company without mentioning one of their all-time classics, the Battlestar Galactica Cylon Bubble Machine. It was a bubble machine shaped like a Cylon – clearly this was a work of unadulterated genius...by your command!

So rack toys played a cherished role in my childhood, and the book you're now holding in your hands proves that I wasn't the only one. Originally intended as cheap throwaway items, they now occupy an important place in the history and collecting of American toys.

Their era has mostly passed, of course, and the world is filled with newer, costlier, and much more sophisticated toys, many of which I also collect and cherish. But I doubt any toys will ever be able to transport me back to that special place of my youth; the toy rack staring back at you right when you walked into the Becket General Store.

Brian Volk-Weiss
Los Angeles, 2020

www.ingramcontent.com/pod-product-compliance
Lightning Source LLC
Chambersburg PA
CBHW042355030426
42336CB00029B/3489